Holy Spirit Power

Holy Spirit Power

Supernatural Encounters That Transform

PENNY WEBSTER

RESOURCE *Publications* • Eugene, Oregon

HOLY SPIRIT POWER
Supernatural Encounters That Transform

Copyright © 2019 Penny Webster. All rights reserved. Except for brief quotations in critical publications or reviews, no part of this book may be reproduced in any manner without prior written permission from the publisher. Write: Permissions, Wipf and Stock Publishers, 199 W. 8th Ave., Suite 3, Eugene, OR 97401.

Resource Publications
An Imprint of Wipf and Stock Publishers
199 W. 8th Ave., Suite 3
Eugene, OR 97401

www.wipfandstock.com

PAPERBACK ISBN: 978-1-5326-9516-2
HARDCOVER ISBN: 978-1-5326-9517-9
EBOOK ISBN: 978-1-5326-9518-6

Manufactured in the U.S.A. 10/17/19

Unless otherwise indicated, all scriptural quotations are from the *New International Version* of the Bible.

Scripture references marked NIV are taken from the HOLY BIBLE, NEW INTERNATIONAL VERSION ®. NIV ®. Copyright © 1973, 1978, 1984 by the International Bible Society. Zondervan.

Scriptures marked KJV are from the King James Version of the Holy Bible.

Scriptures marked NKJV are from the New King James Version of the Holy Bible.

Scriptures marked NASB are from the New American Standard Version of the Holy Bible.

Scriptures marked AMP are from the Amplified Version of the Holy Bible

Scriptures marked ESV are from the English Standard Version of the Holy Bible

Scriptures marked GW are from Gods Word Translation of the Holy Bible Version Trademarks are registered in the United States Patent Office by the International Bible Society

Contents

Introduction | 1

Chapter 1: Answering the Call | 3

Chapter 2: Supernatural Encounters | 15

Chapter 3: Miraculous Missionary Journey | 18

Chapter 4: Supernatural Travel | 26

Chapter 5: Encounter with Jesus | 33

Chapter 6: Courageous Christian | 43

Chapter 7: Under Our Feet | 49

Chapter 8: Fragrance of the Holy Spirit | 56

Chapter 9: Power of the Holy Spirit | 68

Chapter 10: A Life Transformed | 74

Chapter 11: Growing in God | 80

Chapter 12: Where is Your Treasure? | 85

Chapter 13: Exchange Your Battle | 91

Chapter 14: Set Free to Set Others Free | 96

Chapter 15: Jesus Asks a Question | 102

Bibliography | 109

Introduction

GOD ENCOUNTERS, SPECIAL MOMENTS with the creator, something I've experienced since a young child. Each supernatural encounter reveals truth. For over forty years God has been speaking to me. His voice can be found in many ways. God speaks through his word, the Holy Bible. His presence can be found in a song. He inhabits the praises of his people. He reveals himself through creation, in nature. He speaks to our conscience. He speaks to our hearts.

God is not to be put in a box. God can make himself known to anyone, at any time, and in any way he chooses. God reveals himself to those seeking Him. Sometimes he speaks in dreams or visions. God is always speaking; the question is . . . can we hear him? Do we spend time with God, do we set time aside to encounter him? Have we submitted our life to Jesus? Have we invited the Holy Spirit into our lives? Do we spend time in prayer? God is speaking, do we hear him? It can take time to recognize and hear His voice.

For many years, God has shown me things in dreams and visions. I did not always recognize it as God speaking. It took years of seeing things in the supernatural realm before I finally began to see a correlation in each of the encounters he gave. In many years of dreaming, every dream, vision, and encounter I had was different.

After years of experiencing these God moments . . . I prayed and asked God if there was a common element in each of these encounters. After praying, I woke up the next day and had what I like to call a "light bulb moment." It suddenly became clear, almost every encounter had a common thread. The purpose to most everything that Jesus has shown me in dreams has been for the reason of proclaiming good news, healing, and for setting people free. Supernatural encounters, many were given for the purpose of setting the captives free! Almost every experience I've had in the supernatural realm has brought freedom either to myself or to others. We have freedom in Christ. We have been commissioned by God to proclaim freedom to the world around us.

God reveals himself to each person in a different way. Have you ever asked yourself, "What has God called me to do?" Have you ever thought, "What is my purpose in life?" What can I offer to the world around me?" or "How will God use me?"

What is the best way to answer those questions in our lives? The Word of God and supernatural encounters can provide those answers. Let's journey together as we explore some of these encounters given by the power of the Holy Spirit.

"The Spirit of the Sovereign Lord is on me because the Lord has anointed me to proclaim good news to the poor. He has sent me to bind up the brokenhearted to proclaim freedom for the captives and release from darkness for the prisoners, to proclaim the year of the Lord's favor and the day of vengeance of our God, to comfort all who mourn, and provide for those who grieve in Zion—to bestow on them a crown of beauty instead of ashes, the oil of joy instead of mourning, and a garment of praise instead of a spirit of despair."

Isaiah 61: 1–3a
New International Version (NIV)

Chapter 1

Answering the Call

THE PHONE IS RINGING, God is calling. Will you answer? Did you already answer? Have you heard His voice? Do you have a call from God on your life? What is it? Only God knows what your unique calling is. God is calling but what will he say? Receiving that call from God can be exciting but also fearful, what will he ask?

What has God spoken to you? He speaks in different ways to each of us. Before we explore how God has called us personally. Let's first look at how he called those in the bible.

God calls each person in different ways. Some hear His audible voice while others see the call from God with dreams and visions. We all learn differently, and we receive messages from God in different ways. Some people are visual learners, and some are auditory learners. God created each of us, so he knows what learning styles to use when he speaks.

Abram

In the book of Genesis God calls Abram. The "phone rings" and what does he hear from God? The Lord had said to Abram,

> "Go from your country, your people and your father's household to the land I will show you. I will make you into

a great nation, and I will bless you; I will make your name great, and you will be a blessing. I will bless those who bless you, and whoever curses you I will curse, and all peoples on earth will be blessed through you. So Abram went, as the Lord had told him;" Genesis 12:1–4a NIV

Abram had a supernatural encounter when he heard the audible voice of the Lord.

Abram was seventy-five years when he answered the call from God. He listened to the voice of the one who called him. Abram must have been an auditory learner because he heard God.

God is looking for obedience in what he is saying. Abraham is one of the greatest examples in the Bible. God told Abraham to leave his country and he would make him a great nation. What did Abraham do? He did what God told him to do, Abram listened and obeyed.

Joseph

God spoke to Joseph in two dreams!

- *Joseph had a dream, and when he told it to his brothers, they hated him all the more. He said to them, "Listen to this dream I had: We were binding sheaves of grain out in the field when suddenly my sheaf rose and stood upright, while your sheaves gathered around mine and bowed down to it." His brothers said to him, "Do you intend to reign over us? Will you actually rule us?" And they hated him all the more because of his dream and what he had said.*

- *Then he had another dream, and he told it to his brothers. "Listen," he said, "I had another dream, and this time the sun and moon and eleven stars were bowing down to me." When he told his father as well as his brothers, his father rebuked him and said, "What is this dream you had? Will your mother and I and your brothers actually come and bow down to the ground before you?"*

God had great plans for Joseph. He was a man of integrity and honor. He went through much opposition in his life, but God called him to oversee the land of Egypt and to help his family even when they despised him. Joseph knew he had a calling on his life. A calling from God will help keep you strong for many years even in the face of severe opposition.

Joseph was a dreamer, God gave him wisdom in the things he saw. He must have been a visual learner. God spoke to him in his dreams. God helped him to interpret the dreams of others too.

Moses

Moses received the call from God through a burning bush.

> *"So Moses thought, "I will go over and see this strange sight—why the bush does not burn up." When the Lord saw that he had gone over to look, God called to him from within the bush, "Moses! Moses!"*
>
> *And Moses said, "Here I am."*
>
> *"Do not come any closer," God said. "Take off your sandals, for the place where you are standing is holy ground." Then he said, "I am the God of your father, the God of Abraham, the God of Isaac and the God of Jacob." At this, Moses hid his face, because he was afraid to look at God."*
> *(Exodus 3:3-6)*

God called Moses to lead his people the Israelites out of Egypt. Moses was often afraid of his calling, he didn't think he could speak well enough, what would he say, he was full of many questions. Moses had many excuses and doubts. God used Moses mightily even in his weakness! When God calls he delivers! Moses was equipped to do what God called him to do. Why? Because it was God who sent him, it was God who called him. God was with Moses.

Moses must have been a tactile learner. Moses experienced the things of God through touch. God had him to take off his shoes, so he could feel the Holy presence of God where he stood. He experienced the presence of God through the burning bush.

God had him to use what was in his hand. Moses used a staff or rod, and it turned into a serpent, he also used a staff to part the red sea. Moses felt the things of God.

Good News

"Jesus Christ is the same yesterday and today and forever."

Hebrews 13:8 NIV

Since the power of God is the same yesterday, today, and forever we can still experience the miraculous hand of God in our life too.

Do you hear him?

"My sheep hear my voice, and I know them, and they follow me"

John 10:27 KJV

We have the promise in scripture that says we can hear God's voice. "My sheep hear my voice" You were created with the ability to hear from God. There is a still small voice of the Holy Spirit speaking. We listen for God and hear him when we slow down and take time to spend in his presence. You may hear his voice, you may feel his presence, and you may have dreams or visions. God still speaks today and you can "hear" him in many different ways.

"I will instruct you and teach you in the way you should go; I will counsel you with my loving eye on you."

Psalm 32:8 NIV

God is speaking, He longs for a close personal relationship with each of his children. He wants to spend time with us and speak to our hearts. He will instruct us and teach us in the way we should go. (Psalm 32:8) He will release revelation for direction in your life. He will lead you and prepare you for your calling. Trust him

God speaks to everyone differently, but it helps to know in what way you hear from him the most. Knowing your learning style can help if you are beginning to "hear" from God. God speaks and sometimes we might not recognize it. We need to spend quality time with him to hear, see, or feel what he is saying. God continues to speak to his children today, if you do not hear him, maybe you will see him, and if you do not see him then maybe you will feel his presence instead. Sometimes God chooses to reveal himself in all three ways at once!

A Sovereign God

Generally, there are two ways that we can experience a supernatural encounter with the Father, Son, and Holy Spirit. First, we could encounter God in his sovereignty. God can reveal himself sovereignly even to those that aren't seeking him. Sometimes God reveals himself to those who aren't even looking for him. We can see an example of that in the life of Saul mentioned in the bible. Saul was on his way to persecute Christians and Jesus supernaturally revealed himself to him. After Saul encountered Jesus his name was changed to Paul. God has done a complete transformation in his life, so much so, that even his name changed!

Perhaps you have heard testimonies of someone who lived in a remote area or a nation where Christianity is not practiced. Yet, God sovereignly chose to reveal himself to them in a dream or a vision. God can supernaturally show up anywhere and anytime He chooses.

Seeking His Presence

Second, we can seek an encounter with Jesus. Remember the woman with the issue of blood (Matthew 9:20) She said to herself if she could just get to Jesus if she could just enter His presence, she would be made whole. She was seeking Jesus, she pressed through a crowd to get to him, and she reached for Jesus. She encountered Jesus and His healing power! Healing power flowed out of Jesus.

When Jesus lives on the inside of you, you also have Gods anointing flow out of you. When you have opened your life up to God, He can flow through you also. You have been given the power to be His witness.

> *"The Spirit of the Lord is upon me,*
> *because he hath anointed me to preach the gospel to the poor;*
> *he hath sent me to heal the brokenhearted, to preach deliverance to the captives,*
> *and recovering of sight to the blind, to set at liberty them that are bruised,"*
>
> Luke 4:18 KJV

God gives us encounters to serve him. The Spirit of the Lord is upon me. Why? To preach the gospel to the poor. To heal the brokenhearted, to deliver the captives, to bring sight to the blind, and to bring liberty to those that are bruised. If we have asked Jesus to live inside of us, we already have the Holy Spirit living in us. This scripture talks about the Holy Spirit being upon us. When the Holy Spirit comes upon someone they are anointed. They are anointed for the work of the kingdom.

Encounter with the Holy Spirit

I remember the first time I encountered the Holy Spirit as "being upon me." It was during a time of seeking. I was seeking God and seeking direction in my life. I wanted an experience with the Holy Spirit to confirm that God had a ministry plan for my life. When the Holy Spirit came upon someone in the Bible, they became endued with the power to be his witness and to share the gospel with those around them. I wanted to be used by God in ministry, but I also wanted to know that God was with me and that his Holy Spirit power was upon my life. This is what happened. . . .

It was a quiet evening at home. My son was at a friend's house and my husband was at the gym. I was reading a book and studying some scriptures on the Holy Spirit. Many hours I thought about the Holy Spirit. As I was reading, I heard a soft or gentle noise in my house. My window was open, so perhaps the sound came from the wind touching something. I looked over in the direction of the sound, but I didn't see anything. It was a quiet sound, so I kept reading and continued to think about the Holy Spirit. A few seconds later I hear another sound on the floor. This time the sound was a little closer to me. I thought more about what I was hearing. For a quick moment I thought maybe it was the sound of a footstep, but I didn't see anything, and I didn't feel any fear, so I kept reading. My mind was on the Holy Spirit. Then a few seconds after hearing the sound I felt something touch my heart. My heart began to burn it felt like a Holy fire inside me. It was the Holy Spirit. Holy Spirit had been invited into my home, the Holy Spirit walked over to me and touched my heart. After feeling my heart burn for a few minutes I began to cry. The presence of the Holy Spirit was so powerful, and I felt the Holy Spirit in my heart. The Holy Spirit had come upon me. If I had not heard the footstep I wouldn't have realized that the Holy Spirit walked over to me. I'm thankful for hearing, sensing, and feeling the presence of the Holy Spirit.

Soon after the Holy Spirit touched my heart I thought, "The Holy Spirit lives inside of me, why did the Holy Spirit need to walk over to me?" Then I realized the Holy Spirit had come upon me. The Holy Spirit lives inside a believer but the Holy Spirit can also come upon a believer and endue them with power.

It was an encounter with the Holy Spirit that I had been praying for. The Holy Spirit came into the room and walked over to me and touched me and I felt the fire of God burn inside my heart. I cried because the tangible presence of God in my home and in my heart was so intense. As I invited the Holy Spirit in, I could feel the Holy presence of God. The Holy Spirit is with me and upon me.

"And they said to one another, did not our heart burn within us, while he talked with us by the way, and while he opened to us the scriptures?"

Luke 24:32 KJV

Jesus was opening the scriptures to me as I studied and read about the Holy Spirit, I felt the Holy Spirit burn within me also. That evening I couldn't stop thinking about what had happened. I studied scriptures on the Holy Spirit and the power of God showed up. I was seeking an encounter, and I experienced the supernatural power, demonstration, and revelation of the Holy Spirit as he entered my living room.

The Holy Spirit

"But the Helper (Comforter, Advocate, Intercessor—Counselor, Strengthener, Standby), the Holy Spirit, whom the Father will send in my name [in my place, to represent me and act on my behalf], He will teach you all things. And He will help you remember everything that I have told you."

John 14:26 AMP

The Holy Spirit has a mind (Romans 8:27), a will (1 Corinthians 12:11), and emotions (Romans 15:30). The Holy Spirit comforts, strengthens, speaks, and teaches. John 14:26 lists the attributes of the Holy Spirit.

- Comforter
- Advocate
- Intercessor
- Counselor
- Strengthener
- Teacher

Prayer

Welcome, Holy Spirit. You are welcome here. Holy Spirit come into my heart, fill my life, live inside of me and rest upon me. Thank you Holy Spirit for comforting me and for strengthening me. Thank you Holy Spirit for teaching me and guiding me. I pray that everyone reading this book will experience a supernatural encounter with the Holy Spirit. Holy Spirit, I surrender my heart and mind to you. Holy Spirit reveal yourself in my life and empower me to do the work of the kingdom. Holy Spirit fill me, I welcome your presence in my life. Change me and transform my heart to be more like yours. Help me to answer the call you have on my life. I pray in Jesus name Amen.

Responding to the Holy Spirit

When the Holy Spirit comes upon someone they are equipped to minister to others in power of the Holy Spirit.

> *"The Spirit of the Lord is upon me,*
> *because he hath anointed me to preach the gospel to the poor;*
> *he hath sent me to heal the brokenhearted,"*
>
> Luke 4:18a

For years my focus was on God anointing me to preach the gospel to the poor. When I had an encounter with the Holy Spirit my heart opened to see the portion of scripture that also said, "He has sent me to heal the brokenhearted" If the Holy Spirit supernaturally touched my heart and brought healing to me, he could also minister healing to others. The Holy Spirit came upon me to anoint me and send me to also heal the brokenhearted.

The very next day after the fire of the Holy Spirit touched my heart, I went to church. Everything about the church service confirmed what I was hearing from God. The songs were welcoming the Holy Spirit, the preaching was on the Holy Spirit and anointing of God (Luke 4:18), and after church, God connected me with a person who was helping people suffering from depression, anxiety, and insomnia. She shared an opportunity with me to minister to the brokenhearted in the community to overcome depression, anxiety, and insomnia. The Holy Spirit had anointed me the previous evening to send and equip me to minister healing to the brokenhearted in the community. Less than twenty-four hours after the encounter with the Holy Spirit I was being called upon to help the brokenhearted in my community. Praise God! There is healing inside of me because God is within me. An encounter with the Holy Spirit enables you to minister in your area of calling and purpose. Thank you, Holy Spirit!

How will you respond to an encounter?

Divine encounters from the Lord aren't given just to have more head knowledge. The Lord gives us an encounter to experience his presence, to know he is real, and therefore become true witnesses of Jesus.

> *"But the manifestation of the Spirit is given to each one for the profit of all"*
>
> 1 Corinthians 12:7

God wants to give us supernatural encounters, but he also wants us to live in alignment and agreement with what he is saying. When we get a prophetic word or experience an encounter, the Lord is looking for us to participate and be obedient to the things he is saying.

The Lord is calling us to participate in what he is doing. It's up to you. What are you going to do with the word God gives you? What are you going to do with the divine encounter you received? How will you integrate the word of the Lord in our life? Will you share your encounter or just keep it to yourself? Will you be his witness to those around you?

Invite the Holy Spirit in, seek an encounter but be willing to share and act on the things he says through the encounter too.

And Encounter of Heaven

Many years ago my husband had a dream of heaven. The ground where he stood was a sea of glass. There was a sea of people in front of him and to his left and right. Millions of people were standing in front of the throne of God. Way off in the distance he could see a movement of bright colors. His focus was on the people in front of the throne of God, and on the colors way off in the distance, where the throne was. The people were full of joy and excitement, unlike anything you could experience on earth.

He thought, "Wow, I'm standing in front of the throne of God. Look at all these people we made it and we are here worshipping" Then he heard the voice of the Holy Spirit saying, "Turn around" Quickly, my husband's joy and excitement turned to shocked at what he saw behind him. As far as his eye could see was nothing but empty space many times greater than the huge area he had previously seen. It was completely empty. That is when God said, "There is space in front of my throne for everyone I've ever created but most didn't make it" He also said, "Go and tell people."

> *"Also in front of the throne, there was what looked like a sea of glass, clear as crystal."*
>
> *(Revelation 4:6 NIV)*

The Command

God calls us to share His message with everyone so that where he is, they may be also. Go tell people that there is a place in front of His throne. God has made a place for everyone. *"If I go and prepare a place for you, I will come again and receive you to myself, that where I am, there you may be also."* John 14:3 KJV

Be willing to be bendable and changed and challenged. Jesus died for every person on earth. He doesn't see any person as insignificant. Whether they are homeless, or a multi-millionaire God loves them equally. It's about people and believing for souls. Whether they are old and wise or young and without knowledge. God loves them. There have been so many miracles I have seen. The greatest miracle of all is the transformed life. Hope, joy, victory, and strength. The church is supposed to be a witness of this goodness of God in the world.
We are called to be living witnesses. "Go and tell people" He is a miracle working God.

> "He said to them, 'Go into all the world and preach the gospel to all creation. Whoever believes and is baptized will be saved, but whoever does not believe will be condemned.'" (Mark 16:15–16 NIV)

Go into the world and preach the gospel to all creation. There are so many issues and so many viewpoints yet being right or wrong isn't the real issue. It is a matter of life or death. Is a person saved, or will they be condemned? (Mark 16:15–16) That is what matters most. We can bring life to those that need it. Those who hunger and thirst will be fed.

Prayer

Lord Jesus Christ help us to glorify you. God help us to love people, to forgive those that have wronged us. Help us to be faithful and kind. Help us, Jesus, to step out by faith for the things you are asking. Please give us the strength that we need to be living witnesses. Help us to share your truth, words of life, with those that need to hear. Thank you, God, that you answer prayers for your will. May your will be done on earth as it is in heaven. Bring more people into your kingdom and help me to "go and tell people" about you Jesus. Help us to worship you as you deserve Lord Jesus. Use my life to bring more people into your kingdom. In Jesus name, I pray. Amen

Chapter 2

Supernatural Encounters

GOD IS IN THE business of changing hearts! Everything he does has a purpose. I've experienced his miraculous supernatural works first hand. True God encounters change hearts and transform lives. He has done much through my life and yet I want to be very careful to give all the glory to God. I want to be clear that the experiences I'm about to share are not to be sought after. Only God is the one to be sought after. Only by the Holy Spirit did these things occur. Prayer works. I did nothing on my own to cause them to happen.

> *"Not by might, nor by power, but by my spirit, saith the Lord of hosts"*
>
> *Zechariah 4:6b KJV*

Several years ago, while serving in children's ministry . . . a church member gave me a book to read. I had no idea how much that book would impact my life. The book was called "Children and the Supernatural."[1] The book spoke of children being used by God. It gave real accounts of kids being used by God through visions, healings, and miracles.

---

1. Toledo, *Children and the Supernatural*, 38–40.

The children were touched by God in various ways. God did a supernatural work in many of their lives. However, there was one encounter that stood out to me more so than the others. The Holy Spirit touched my heart in a special way as I read about a children's church service.

The young children could feel the tangible presence of God. Some kids were weeping, some were on their knees praying and others were on their backs. Many children began to have visions. The presence of God was so intense that one little girl stayed for hours after the church had ended. She remained at the altar as God was doing a mighty work in her life. She would cry and then stop for a while. She would laugh and then cry again. Her parents knew God was at work and didn't want to interrupt. They patiently waited until their child got up from the altar. When the young child got up, she was shaking from her experience. She then gave a long-detailed account of her encounter with God.

First, God washed her sins away, then He told her that He had a beautiful and holy calling for her life. He showed her many things, He spoke about a land, about the people, the government and the economy. She was only seven years old, yet she described events as though she was an expert with a political science degree. The Lord told her that He would pour out His Spirit on the land again and that one day he would send her there, but for now, he wanted her to pray. The parents asked if their child remembered the name of the place she was shown. The young child answered, "Have you ever heard of a place called North Korea?" Without even knowing a place called North Korea exist she gave the most accurate revelation of how to pray for the government and people.

As I read her testimony, my knowledge of North Korea was limited. Until reading that book, I never even thought about North Korea or its people. Yet, as I read about her encounter with God, He placed a supernatural love in my heart for that young child, a missionary, and for the people of North Korea. God touched my heart as I thought about her experience with him. My heart began to break for the people of North Korea and I just wanted to pray over the little girl. She had been commissioned by God and was told to pray. Yet, how many people were praying for her? I suddenly felt an urgent call to pray for the protection of that child.

I was given the book as a gift because I serve in children's ministry. It was written by someone who I could identify with, another children's minister. However, I knew the reason God had placed the book in my hands was so that I could pray specifically for that child. Here I was, a children's minister, reading about a child, who would one day go to North Korea. The most dangerous place in the world for a Christian to be.

I quickly turned the pages to find out when the book was released. It was published in 2012. I could only estimate how old she might be by now. What if she was touched by God a few years prior to the publication? I could only guess it happened a few years before the book was released. If so, she could be as young as 14 years old or could be an adult already. How could I know? Was I too late? Did I have time to pray for the protection of that missionary before she was sent into North Korea? Was she there already? All I could do was pray. I knew my purpose for receiving that book, such a beautiful gift, was to pray for that missionary. So, I did, I prayed.

A few nights later, I had a supernatural encounter myself. I was not seeking an encounter, it just suddenly happened because God was doing a work in my life. I had only prayed for North Korea a few times. I don't remember asking God to take me to North Korea, I just remember praying for North Korean missionaries. Yet, I truly believe, with all my heart, that God supernaturally allowed me to visit North Korea one evening. Little did I know after reading that book that the Lord would also show me North Korea. He did a work through my life that only He could have done. He made possible something that would have been impossible any other way.

Chapter 3

Miraculous Missionary Journey

ONE NIGHT, AS I went to sleep, I had no idea that God had a miraculous missionary journey planned out for me. God transported me to North Korea! I was not having a dream, it was not a vision, by the power of the Holy Spirit I was supernaturally transported over six thousand miles away. Whether in the body or out of the body, I do not know. One minute I was in North Carolina, and the next minute I was in North Korea. I traveled by the power of the Holy Spirit by divine appointment.

Suddenly, by the Spirit, I supernaturally descended from the sky. I was high enough to be able to look over a grassy area the size of a football field. I could see someone standing in a field and before I knew it God had placed me right beside a person who was hiding in some tall grass. Before landing in the grass, I could see a person, possibly a guard, standing close to the border.

As I landed, it startled the person hiding in the grass next to me. I sensed her fear as she hid in the grass. It was clear to me that she was hiding because she was crouched down, in the grass above her head, with a look of fear on her face. I could sense the intense fear she was experiencing. She was on my left side and I was her right. I believe God specifically placed me there, on her right side. I had not chosen where to land, I was supernaturally placed in that exact spot beside her.

She knew the North Korean guards were nearby. Perhaps she had prayed for guidance and direction and I was sent there by God, as an answer to that prayer. Although she was extremely frightened, I also sensed that her fear had diminished some while I sat next to her. My presence had comforted her if even just a little bit. I didn't speak the language and without communicating I instinctively knew how she felt. I also knew what needed to be done. I was sent to North Korea to help protect her and allow her to escape that area of danger. Perhaps she was trying to cross the border into safe territory.

I knew the guard's surrounding her needed to be distracted. Somehow their attention needed to be away from her so it would enable her to escape. What could I do? My plan was to make noises and stay put so the guards could find me instead. I would make sounds while letting her escape without them hearing her. I would be like a sitting duck allowing the guards to come towards me instead. In the meantime, I would be giving her time to escape. I did not communicate my plan with her before I made a sound. I only began by making a clicking noise. She shook her head no, with a look of terror at the first sound I made. She didn't want the guards to find her. No wonder she was terrified as I began to make a sound.

God had strategically placed me on her right side to shield her from the guard on her right. I motioned or pointed with my left hand towards the left, the direction she would be heading, she looked at my hand and she left, just as I had pointed for her to do so. She quietly went in the direction I pointed to, while I stayed still in the grass. I continued making noises. There was a guard standing somewhere on the right side and I knew it wouldn't take him long to find me.

As the guard approached me, he began yelling. I believe he was telling the other guards that he found someone. I can only guess what he was saying but as he was yelling it made even more noise. The more noise that was being made the better. Now, the guards were focusing on him, which gave my friend a few extra moments to escape without being seen. Knowing that all the guards were focusing in one place brought me great joy as my friend had more time to escape. She would be set free.

The guard walked up to me and immediately grabbed me by the throat. A normal person would have been intimidated at that moment. My throat was being grabbed as if to say shut up. However, I was so happy my friend escaped that I couldn't contain my joy. I wasn't even frightened by the guard, I was just smiling at what had happened. I looked into the guard's eyes and he looked at me as though I was an alien from outer space. He was completely shocked, he was frightened in my presence. I was not afraid, He was. He had never seen anyone like me before. As he grabbed me by the throat, I was smiling and as I felt peace and happiness for setting someone free. I did not feel any fear, I only felt compassion for him. I knew he did not understand peace or happiness. It is as though I could feel the Father Gods heart of compassion towards him. He had never experienced joy and had never seen anyone who was genuinely happy until that moment.

He was shocked by what he was seeing. I could tell he had never seen anyone like me before. I don't think he had ever seen an American before. He had tried to frighten me, but he was the one that became frightened instead. He had probably never seen anyone with red hair, or blue eyes. I'm not exactly sure what he was seeing, maybe he saw angels behind me backing me up? Maybe I appeared as a spiritual being only? All I know is he looked very shocked as I looked at him and smiled. I think it puzzled him that I had even smiled. I could tell he did not understand peace or happiness. Jesus is the only source of happiness. Jesus is the only source of peace. I was full of joy as I instinctively knew that the person that I was sent to rescue had made it to safety. It was then that I woke up or came back to North Carolina.

By the power of the Holy Spirit, I had traveled to North Korea and helped to set someone free from its oppressive land. Could it have been a missionary? Could it have been the very same missionary I was praying for? I don't know. I just know that it was a supernatural experience that was very real to me. God could have used anyone, but he chose to use me, an ordinary person. God touched my heart for the people of North Korea and he used me supernaturally to make a difference through prayer and through a supernatural event. God could have used that encounter as a way of showing me how my prayers were being answered. He personally allowed me to experience the moment of her freedom!

Confirmation after an Encounter

This is not the first time that God has supernaturally taken me to other locations far away. Each time He has done something supernatural in my life, He confirms it with natural things shortly thereafter. Each time, it is only by the power of the Holy Spirit that they occur. They were completely unexpected and happened all in Gods timing.

God often allows me to receive confirmation and proof afterward such supernatural experiences occur. God helps me understand that it was, in fact, God, and not just my imagination. No sooner did that experience happen, and my husband walked in the room. As he walked in the room, I said, "You're not going to believe what just happened to me." Before I could finish my sentence, my husband said, "I was just watching a television show on North Korea." Then, he shared a few quick comments on his opinion towards the leadership of North Korea.

What a comment to hear first thing when I get back from my surprise missionary visit to North Korea! Before I could even mention or say anything about North Korea, the first sentence that came out of my husband's mouth was about North Korea. To understand just how amazing that is. . . . Just know that in over 25 years of marriage, we have never even spoken about North Korea that I can ever remember. We never, ever talked about North Korea and suddenly, I hear the words "North Korea" the moment I get ready to share what happened. Incredible!

More Confirmation

I received more confirmation from God the following day as I watched a program on North Korea. The documentary showed an area with tall grass near the North Korean border. As I looked at the tall grass, I knew in my heart I had been there the day before. It was true. God took me to North Korea and used me, an ordinary person to do an extraordinary thing, to free someone, perhaps it was a missionary. Could it have been the same missionary I had prayed for? God only knows. Thank you, Jesus Wherever the Spirit of the Lord is, there is freedom!

"Now the Lord is the Spirit, and where the Spirit of the Lord is, there is freedom."

2 Corinthians 3:17

"The Spirit of the Lord is on me because he has anointed me to proclaim good news to the poor. He has sent me to proclaim freedom for the prisoner and recovery of sight for the blind, to set the oppressed free"

Luke 4:18

"Not by might nor by power, but by my Spirit,' says the Lord Almighty."

Zechariah 4:6b

There is more attached to your obedience to God than just your obedience. Your prayer is linked to someone's breakthrough, someone's salvation, someone's healing, someone's freedom, or someone's deliverance. Your prayer can be linked to a nationwide or worldwide revival. God is calling us to the heart of the Father and to prayer. God is waiting for us to get our hearts right. He is waiting on us to align our hearts with his. He is waiting for us to enter his presence. He is waiting for us to agree with him and to partner with him to set people free.

Heart Transformation

When supernatural encounters are given they often result in transformation or a change of heart. Your see, before that encounter, I did not think about North Korea. Now, my heart is tender towards the people of North Korea. Encounters have a way of taking the focus off of ourselves and they bring glory to God. Only God can change a heart. Only he can set a person free. Only he can transform a life. Only God can touch a heart in a way that will cause a person to pray in an area they had never even previously thought about. Only he can supernaturally transport a person to an area that would otherwise be off limits. Often, the result of a supernatural encounter is change.

God is not limited by time or space!

God is not limited by time or space. He can do anything, through any person, at any time. He answers prayer! There is power in prayer. There is no distance too great or situation too impossible that He cannot change. God protects his people. There are no limitations on prayer. Your prayers can travel any distance. Thank you, Jesus, Thank you!

I am still learning how to pray for and help the people in North Korea. If you would also like to pray for North Korea and other places around the world you can visit the Operation World website for a daily prayer guide. I've also found an organization that helps the persecuted Christians in North Korea. I plan on writing a few letters of encouragement to the Christians in Korea. God has changed my heart for that land, and for the people of North Korea. My heart breaks for them and for all their suffering. All I know to do for now, is to pray for the people.

Holy Spirit Power

Sometimes it seems like such a small thing to do. To just pray. However, one small act of obedience can make a huge impact on others. What would have happened if my friend had never given me that book to read? I would not have been praying for missionaries in North Korea. My prayers would not have traveled to North Korea. God uses ordinary people in extraordinary ways. Listen to his voice and obey his leading. God uses willing vessels. Maybe he will have you give to someone, maybe he will have you pray for someone, and maybe he will send you on a missionary journey. Maybe he will do a supernatural work in your heart. You never know the impact that one small act of obedience can have in your life and in the lives of others around you.

"He upholds the cause of the oppressed and gives food to the hungry. The Lord sets prisoners free."

Psalm 146:7 New International Version

"I tell you, open your eyes and look at the fields! They are ripe for harvest"

John 4:35b NIV

Prayer

Lord Jesus, I pray that you bring freedom to North Korea. I pray for freedom of religion. I pray that the Holy Spirit would be welcome in North Korea. I pray for protection and for resources. God, please protect their faith. Help the people with the food shortage. God help them with your hand, release believers who have been imprisoned, and please restore them. Holy Spirit, please bring comfort and strengthen all those in need. Protect the missionaries you have sent and help them to share the gospel and bring light and hope to even the most difficult situations. I pray that you raise up intercessors for North Korea. Jesus, please reveal yourself to the North Korean people in dreams and visions. Give them hope, comfort, and strength for each day by the power of the Holy Spirit. Amen

Chapter 4

Supernatural Travel

Is TRAVELING IN THE spirit scriptural? Yes, there are many examples we can look at in scripture. The idea of traveling in the spirit can be a controversial subject. I must be clear that I am referring only to the Holy Spirit. Only by the power of the Holy Spirit do these things occur. Only on Gods schedule do they happen. We don't seek after power, we only seek after Jesus. These are not everyday events however they can happen when God chooses. The Bible is full of examples of dreams, visions, and miracles.

The enemy tries to distort the things of God. I'm not speaking of dark forces, new age ideas, human efforts, and things that are not biblically based. That is not what I am talking about. I want to speak only on scriptural encounters that are biblically based in the one and only true living God.

We can see from the Holy Scriptures that God transported people in the Bible. If God did it then, He can do it now, if and when He chooses. Although, it isn't something that we often hear about. The scripture does teach us, it happens! It can happen.

Look at John 6:16-21 *"When evening came, his disciples went down to the lake, where they got into a boat and set off across the lake for Capernaum. By now it was dark, and Jesus had not yet joined them. A strong wind was blowing, and the waters grew rough. When they had rowed about three or four miles, they saw Jesus approaching*

Supernatural Travel

the boat, walking on the water; and they were frightened. But he said to them, "It is I; don't be afraid." Then they were willing to take him into the boat, and immediately the boat reached the shore where they were heading."

Jesus and the disciples were supernaturally transported! The Sea of Galilee is eight miles across. If the boat had traveled three or four miles, it is safe to say that the disciples were in the middle of the sea. Jesus immediately transported them to the shore, four or five miles away. When Jesus entered the boat, their vessel, they immediately arrived at their destination. In an instant, God supernaturally took them to the shore.

Holy Spirit is everything we need, he is a counselor, comforter, and if needed, he will get us to where we need to be supernaturally. In the middle of a storm, Jesus made a surprise appearance to the disciples. In an instant, Jesus supernaturally moved the boat and all the disciples in it.

Read Acts 8:36-40 *"As they traveled along the road, they came to some water and the eunuch said, "Look, here is water. What can stand in the way of my being baptized?" And he gave orders to stop the chariot. Then both Philip and the eunuch went down into the water and Philip baptized him. When they came up out of the water, the Spirit of the Lord suddenly took Philip away, and the eunuch did not see him again but went on his way rejoicing. Philip, however, appeared at Azotus and traveled about, preaching the gospel in all the towns until he reached Caesarea."*

Philip was filled with faith and the Holy Spirit. Scripture teaches that it was "the Spirit of the Lord" that transported Philip. He was divinely guided and miraculously transported north, over thirty miles away. As soon as Philip completed his task to baptize the Eunuch he was suddenly taken away. Once the good news of Jesus was shared with an Ethiopian who repented and was baptized, Philip was needed elsewhere.

The Spirit of the Lord took Philip where he needed to be. Jesus is serious about reaching the lost and using us to do it. The Spirit of the Lord can position a person in the right place and at the right time to help another person during a time of need. Yes, the Spirit of the Lord is able to supernaturally transport a person so that they may do the work of the kingdom.

Each day we step out and do the work of the kingdom and if necessary the Holy Spirit will work as a supernatural airline pilot. The Holy Spirit is not my co-pilot, he is the pilot. He decides where I go, he is in charge. He leads me and knows what direction to take. Philip was completely yielded to the Holy Spirit. The Holy Spirit will get you to where you need to be if you are willing to go. He will do the work and make sure you do not miss a divine appointment. He will take you where he wants you to be. When you follow a God who is not limited in any way, you can do the impossible! If he did it for Philip he could do the same today for you and me.

We say we want to be used by God and we give our lives to him but often we ask him to make our plans work out for us. Instead, we need to surrender our plans and daily lives to him and allow him to use us as he wants. He won't take you out of the driver's seat by force. God wants us to surrender our will to his will. He wants to lead us and guide us and take us to where he wants us to be. God acts through people to affect the world around us.

If God has the power to literally move a person to another location, surely he can give us visions of other places by the power of the Holy Spirit. God can do anything.

See Ezekiel 8:1-4 *"It came about in the sixth year, on the fifth day of the sixth month, as I was sitting in my house with the elders of Judah sitting before me, that the hand of the Lord God fell on me there. Then I looked, and behold, a likeness as the appearance of a man; from His loins and downward there was the appearance of fire, and from His loins and upward the appearance of brightness, like the appearance of glowing metal. He stretched out the form of a hand and caught me by a lock of my head; and the Spirit lifted me up between earth and heaven and brought me in the visions of God to Jerusalem, to the entrance of the north gate of the inner court, where the seat of the idol of jealousy, which provokes to jealousy, was located. And behold, the glory of the God of Israel was there, like the appearance which I saw in the plain."*

Supernatural Travel

Ezekiel is lifted into the sky by the power of the Holy Spirit. Scripture says "the hand of the Lord fell upon Ezekiel." It was the hand of God that took hold of Ezekiel and the Spirit lifted him up in a vision. Ezekiel is taken up and transported to Jerusalem. God shows him abominations, sinful, wicked and evil things, idolatry in Jerusalem. Visions can also be given at times to reveal hidden things or evil in various places.

One minute Ezekiel is sitting in his house talking with the elders the next minute he is seeing Jerusalem. God sees everything and he has the ability to allow us to see what he is seeing too. God may provide a vision or he may lift you up by the power of his Spirit as he did with Ezekiel. As you stay connected with the Holy Spirit you get to see what he sees and go where he goes.

When we are one with Christ Jesus we can see what he sees. Do you think Jesus sees his children? Do you think God sees the poor? Do you think God sees the hurting? Do you think he sees the abused? Do you think he sees sin and wickedness? Do you think God sees the broken- hearted? God sees everything and he can reveal anything to you at any time. Sometimes he will reveal hidden things so that you can intercede or effectively pray for change.

Ezekiel 40:1-2 *"In the twenty-fifth year of our exile, at the beginning of the year, on the tenth of the month, in the fourteenth year after the fall of the city—on that very day the hand of the Lord was on me and he took me there. In visions of God he took me to the land of Israel and set me on a very high mountain, on whose south side were some buildings that looked like a city." He took me there, and I saw a man whose appearance was like bronze; he was standing in the gateway with a linen cord and a measuring rod in his hand."*

Ezekiel has another vision from God, he is taken to Israel and God sets him on a high mountain. God took him there and God set him there. The hand of the Lord was upon Ezekiel. God will pour out His Spirit on all people! Is supernatural travel possible? Yes. Do we do anything to control it? No. Scripture says that it is only by the hand of the Lord Jesus. It is only by the Holy Spirit that these things occur. Scripture says that it is God that set Ezekiel on that mountain.

God is pouring out his spirit on his servants, He is pouring out his Spirit on all people. Almighty God can do whatever he wants in order to reach those who need him.

> *"I will pour out my Spirit on all people.*
> *Your sons and daughters will prophesy,*
> *your young men will see visions,*
> *your old men will dream dreams.*
> *Even on my servants, both men, and women,*
> *I will pour out my Spirit in those days,*
> *and they will prophesy.*
> *I will show wonders in the heavens above*
> *and signs on the earth below. . . ."*

Supernatural Sight, Vision 400 miles away!

My husband and I have served in children's ministry for twelve years at Evangel Worship Center in North Carolina. Before God originally called my family to North Carolina he gave me a supernatural vision of the church we would be serving in. Thirteen years ago, my family was living in Maryland and yet God showed me a vision of a church sanctuary in North Carolina. In the vision God gave me, I could see in great detail the area surrounding the pulpit. Incredible. By the power of the Holy Spirit I had seen a room, the exact room in North Carolina I would be ministering in. At the time God gave me the vision in Maryland, I was over 400 miles away from the church building in North Carolina. In a vision, and by the power of the Holy Spirit, God showed me in great detail where my family would be serving in ministry.

The very first time my husband and I visited our church in North Carolina I said, "I've already been here. God showed me this exact room already, this is where God wants us to be." We faithfully served twelve years at that location. The vision God gave of that church sanctuary kept me going during the difficult times. I knew beyond a shadow of a doubt that I was right where God wanted me to be. Since God provided that vision, I could be confident that he was with me. Jesus had gone before me and prepared the way. The hand of the Lord had placed me there. I'm so thankful for that vision. It was given by God during a time where I was seeking him for the next step of ministry in my family's life. Visions from God can often bring wisdom and direction.

God does not use anyone in ministry until they have had an encounter with God, or they have been anointed to do the work of the kingdom first. Sure there are people who try to minister in their own strength but an encounter and anointing from God are what brings ministry to life, Jesus is life, He will keep you going when things get difficult, and when obstacles happen.

God used supernatural encounters in the bible when he called his servants to do the work of the kingdom, and God still uses supernatural encounters today. I know this to be true.

Supernatural Travel 2,000 miles away!

One evening, by the power of the Holy Spirit, God supernaturally took me to Utah. I was in North Carolina at the time it happened. My daughter had moved to Utah and I was heart-broken. Yet, God allowed me to supernaturally travel to Utah so that I could see exactly what was happening in my daughter's life. This was not a dream, instead God Almighty allowed my spirit to supernaturally travel to Utah and see for myself what was happening. My daughter was in a room with some "friends." They were smoking and trying to talk her into making an unhealthy decision. I was able to take a stand in the spiritual realm against the negative influences in her life. God allowed me to see her situation. He showed me exactly what was happening in her life, at that very moment, so that I could pray for her protection.

How do I know that God really transported me to Utah to see my daughter? I know because the following day my daughter posted something on Facebook and it confirmed exactly what I had seen the evening before. My God is amazing. Only by the power of the Holy Spirit could I have traveled 2,000 miles away to see my daughter so I could pray for her in a time of need. Only by the power of God could I have entered into the very room she was in. My body was in North Carolina but my eyes were clearly seeing a room in Utah. The Holy Spirit took me to Utah to pray for my daughter.

This experience shows me that God cares so much about each and every one of us. God can reveal things to us by the power of the Holy Spirit that we wouldn't know any other way. Supernatural encounters are often given for insight on how to pray effectively for breakthrough and freedom. God is not limited by time, space or distance. He can show you anything, anywhere and at any time. He is amazing! Thank you, Jesus, for releasing supernatural keys of wisdom and insight by the power of the Holy Spirit.

Chapter 5

Encounter with Jesus

The Battle for Souls

THERE IS A BATTLE in the spirit realm for the salvation of souls. For years I prayed for a family member who did not know Jesus. The more I prayed the worse it got. All I could do was pray because I lacked wisdom on how to best share the gospel with him. I struggled on how to convey the message of Christ in a way that could be understood and accepted in that person's life. I did what I could to avoid confrontation. I was a peacemaker, not a debater. However, he was great at debating points of unbelief, and would sometimes confront me about my beliefs.

I always felt inadequate to share the gospel with him. The more I mentioned Jesus to him the angrier and more hostile he became. He would say things such as "You only believe because you've been brainwashed since a young child" I didn't know how to respond to his comments. It was like being ambushed with an arsenal of negative comments and disbelief. My only weapon was prayer. All I was able to do was pray. I didn't have the strength or ability to make a difference with persuading words, and I didn't yet understand my authority in Christ. Only God could change his heart.

I couldn't prove my faith in a way that made sense to him. It was the first time that my faith had been under such an attack, I didn't know how to defend myself or my faith. I am thankful that I didn't need to because God is my defense!

My defense is of God, who saves the upright in heart.

Psalm 7:10

The Evening Jesus Appeared

That night, I cried out to God like never before. I went to bed in despair. My faith had been under such an attack that I began to question my very own beliefs. I was taught about Jesus at a young age and I had seen him do many things in my life. Yet, I needed to know beyond a shadow of a doubt that God was real. I prayed with tears streaming down my face. I was seeking God for myself. I needed to know that Jesus was real and not because someone else had told me about him early in life. I needed to know for myself that Jesus was real. How could I continue sharing Jesus with others when I couldn't even prove He existed? So, I cried out in prayer repeatedly asking God to reveal himself to me, "Jesus are your real? I've been through some difficulty, God are you real?" I've prayed for years and years for this person's salvation and it only seems to get worse. God are you real? I was told at a young age about you but I need to know for myself. God are you real? Jesus are you real? Help me Jesus, Help me I don't have the right words to say to prove you exist. I need your help, Jesus. I can't do this without your help. Please God, how can I know that you are real?"

"Then you will call on me and come and pray to me, and I will listen to you. You will seek me and find me when you seek me with all your heart. I will be found by you," declares the Lord" Jeremiah 29:12-14a NIV

Encounter with Jesus

The Moment Jesus Appears

Suddenly my eyes opened to the spiritual realm. I could hear and see two white doves flying off to my right side, as the doves flew to the right they slowly disappeared into the glory of the Lord. Jesus himself appeared to me. My eyes had been opened to Him and I could see Jesus in my room. Jesus was above me and He lovingly reached out His arms toward me. As I looked up to Jesus He was smiling at me. Light was emanating from him, he is light, a brilliant light of glory, a pure light that gives life, love, and revelation. I could see the features of his face enough to recognize it as Jesus. The light of Jesus shines bright and he looked transparent at the same time. In other words, I could see his features but they were seen through light and not seen with flesh. As I looked to Jesus I felt love, compassion, peace, and concern for me.

My First Thoughts When I see Him

As soon as I was in the presence of Jesus all my worries evaporated. My concerns disappeared and all I could focus on was Jesus. As my worries vanished in His presence I thought to myself, "Oh, Lord please forgive me, how can I be so selfish thinking about problems that don't even exist. I should be focusing on the pain that you endured on the cross for me. Why am I concentrating on myself when I should be totally focused on you, Jesus."

Thoughts Speak As Loud As Words

As I pondered those thoughts I was aware that the Lord heard them completely. I realized in the spirit realm, our thoughts speak just as loud as our words. He knows every thought. I simply thought something and he knew what I was thinking. Although Jesus heard my thoughts about him, he did not respond because they would draw attention to himself. Jesus was focusing his attention on me. He is humble and he puts the concerns of others first. His concern was for me. So, Jesus asked me something.

The Moment Jesus Speaks

Jesus looked right at me. And although I do not remember the exact words he spoke. He did ask me a question. He lovingly looked at me and asked something like, "What are you crying about?" or perhaps He said, "What is wrong?" He could have said, "What is bothering you?" All I remember is that Jesus himself was responding to the cries of my heart. Jesus wanted to know about the things that were troubling me. He wanted to hear the concerns of my heart. Jesus asked me a question and he was there to listen. He wanted to hear from me. It is so amazing that such a loving God would take the time to hear from me. I can talk to him anytime and he genuinely wants to listen to me and my concerns. That is so amazing to experience. I'm so thankful for heartfelt communication with the Savior. Thank you, Jesus.

My Response

It was difficult to think about problems while in the presence of Jesus. All the worries seemed to immediately fade away while in his presence, and yet Jesus asked me a question about what was bothering me. I had to answer Jesus. What should I tell him? Talk about a dream come true. I'm literally face-to-face with Jesus and he asks me what's wrong or what he can do to help. I could have asked him for anything.

I struggled to remember what I had been crying about just moments before He appeared. It was hard to recall problems when the answer to all problems is right there with you. For a quick moment I thought, "I'm with Jesus I could ask him for anything maybe I should ask Him for a healing" then I thought, "Wait a minute, Jesus already paid the price for my healing, in the spirit realm I understood that I was already healed."

Then I remembered, I was believing God for the salvation of a family member. I had been praying that God would save his soul. I don't remember what I said to Jesus but I do remember answering his question. I am not able to recall the conversation we had.

I just know that I shared my heart and he listened and comforted me.

He Covers Me

After Jesus and I spoke he took a blanket and covered me. He told me to rest. I am his child and he just wanted me to rest in his presence. I could rest knowing that he had heard my cries and I had given him my concerns. After you hand over your concerns to Jesus you can rest knowing he will take care of you. He is your Father and he will cover you.

Jesus Listens

I felt an overwhelming peace and love in his presence, a brilliant light of glory. He himself is light, not just a light that illuminates but a light of knowledge, a light of understanding.

> "O Lord, you are my light; yes, Lord, you light up my darkness" (2 Samuel 22:29 NLT)

God heard my cry and he answered! He wants us to come to him as we are. He is not bothered by our brokenness or even by our questioning his existence. He is happy when we call on his name.

> *"The Lord is close to the brokenhearted and saves those who are crushed in spirit"*
>
> *Psalm 34:18 NIV*

God spent time with me, He listened to me and comforted me, and then he covered me and told me to rest. He just wants us to rest in his presence. Resting in God is important. Remember to take time to slow down and enjoy his presence. More can be accomplished by resting in God than by many hours of effort or striving. Make time to rest in his presence.

Jesus is amazing when we tell him our worries all we need to do is rest. We can rest knowing that he heard us and that the battle isn't ours, it belongs to him, the Lord. We hand him our pain, our cares, our concerns, and he takes them away, then we can rest knowing he has provided the answer. Certainly, he wants to bring salvation to the lost. He is listening, He will answer your cry. He loves you, he wants to know the things on your heart and mind. He wants to draw close to you, he wants to hear from you, and to give you rest.

Draw near to God and He will draw near to you.

James 4:8 NKJV

The Lord is a refuge for the oppressed, a stronghold in times of trouble. Those who know your name will trust in you, for you, Lord, have never forsaken those who seek you.

Psalm 9:9-10 NIV

Transformation

Change of Perspective, From Sorrow to Peace

In His presence, all things change. There is joy and peace in his presence. My perspective completely changed in his presence. Why was I worrying about earthly concerns when I should have been focusing on Jesus? One minute I'm crying my heart out, with feelings of despair and the next moment I'm in his presence and every concern disappears. The only thing that mattered was him. The only thing worth thinking about was him. The only thing I wanted to do was praise him and do more for him to give him glory. There is peace in his presence.

"Cast all your anxiety on him because he cares for you."

1 Peter 5:7 NIV

Encounter with Jesus

"You will keep him in perfect peace, whose mind is stayed on You, Because he trusts in You."

Isaiah 26:3 NKJV

In his presence I was unable to dwell on my pain I was only able to see hope. He is my hope. I just looked up to Jesus, into a heavenly realm, where all things are possible. I was looking at Jesus, keeping your eyes on Jesus will change your perspective. Looking to Jesus changed my perspective from sorrow, problems and worry to answers, peace and rest. The Holy Spirit revealed to me things that I had not been able to see a moment before in my earthly state of thinking. I just needed to communicate my concerns with Jesus and He is there to listen and give me rest.

Love Transforms

What an experience to be face to face with love itself, to be with the King of kings, the Lord of lords, the Alpha and Omega, the great I AM. It is pleasing to know that Almighty God cares so very much about us. There is no such thing as a problem in the sight of the Lord. Nothing is too big or too complicated for him to handle. No problem is too small for it to be mentioned, He cares about everything small concerns and large ones. Yet, every concern we have is so tiny when we compare it to the mighty power of God. It comforts me to know that God is interested in our smallest concern. He wants to be invited into all things great and small. He is a wonderful counselor, he is a best friend and a friend you can feel comfortable sharing anything with. I do not feel any condemnation in his presence. I only feel acceptance, reassurance, concern, comfort, wholeness, and love—an unconditional love that is never ending and without limits.

I thank God for his transforming power. I have forever been changed by those moments with Jesus. Is God real? Yes, He is! In his presence, there is peace, hope, joy, love, understanding, revelation, and rest. You can trust God. He will set you free from any challenge you are facing. All things are possible with him. Just believe. Have faith and trust in him and he will lead you to victory! He is victorious. In Christ Jesus, we are also victorious.

> *"But I trust in your unfailing love; my heart rejoices in your salvation. I will sing to the Lord for he has been good to me"*
>
> Psalm 13:5-6 NIV

The presence of God is so powerful. While in his presence, I am more aware that my relationship always needs to be close to him. When you are face to face with the living God there is nothing else. All priorities change. Earthly concerns diminish and the desire to worship him intensifies. He is the only thing of importance. It is my desire to be thankful to him for all he has done for me. The Lord is worthy of praise.

Transformation Continues as Salvations Follow

This experience not only changed my life.... I am happy to say that the person I had been praying for is now saved. Thank you, Jesus. Shortly after my encounter with Jesus, the person I was praying for called on God to save his soul. Four years after he invited God into his life, he went to Bible College, he has served in children's ministry for twelve years, he has become an elder in the church, and he also helps with prison ministry too. God not only answered my prayer to save him, but God used his life to save the lives of others as well. I believe many more lives were saved in the years following his salvation.

Praise God, there is nothing more important to God than the salvation of souls. Only He can change a heart of unbelief into one that is transformed and believes in Him. Only he can bring freedom. Only He can change a heart from one that spews hatred towards God into one that partners with God and shares the gospel with others. Only God can save souls, yet he chooses everyday regular people to testify of his goodness to others. Glory to God.

God is in the business of changing hearts and transforming lives! Keep praying. God hears your prayers. Prayers make an enormous impact in the kingdom of God.

Never the Same Again

I've seen Jesus and I've never been the same. We are all called to share Jesus with others, with family, friends, co-workers, and community. Pray, and never give up. Your prayers make a difference. When Jesus appears hearts are changed.

Jesus stands at the door of our heart waiting for us to let him in. "Here I am! I stand at the door and knock. If anyone hears my voice and opens the door, I will come in" Revelation 3:20 NIV God is with us whether we feel him or not, he is always near. Perhaps you know him already, or maybe you are not sure if he is real. Perhaps you don't yet believe, if you seek him you will find him. You will never be the same again. The people you pray for, once they encounter Jesus, they will never be the same either!

Prayer

Jesus, there is nothing more important than salvation. There is nothing more important than knowing you and having a relationship with you and having the ability to hear from you. I thank you for giving your life on the cross and shedding your blood for the forgiveness of my sins. You not only died but you rose again. You defeated death, hell, and the grave. You are the living God and I pray that those who don't know you would ask you to enter their life and make them new.

Thank you for hearing my prayers and for saving my family. God, it is your will that none should perish and all should come to repentance. Touch hearts that are hard and soften them to receive from you. Save the lost, open their eyes that they might see their need for salvation. God, you accept all into your family if they will only call upon your name. I pray that those who do not know you would call upon your name and be saved. Jesus, only you can turn a hard heart into one that is open to receive you. Jesus, open hearts to receive you I pray. In Jesus Name. Amen

Chapter 6

Courageous Christian

WE HAVE BEEN GIVEN power and authority by God. When we trust in his word, he gives us supernatural courage and boldness. Even when problems double up or may appear twice our size, we have been given the power to overcome by using the word of God. With God on our side, we always have the victory. Watch and see what the Lord did to reveal this truth.

The Army of the Lord

When my son was just seven years old, I witnessed him do something incredible. While my son, Christian, was playing outside I was watching him from a distance. He went outside carrying a sword and had on the full armor of God. He was wearing camouflaged army pants, his shirt had a picture of a Bible, a shield, and a belt of truth. He and another young child were both holding swords. They were sword fighting.

Two teenagers that were twice Christian's age got close to him attempting to frighten him. They were much taller than my son. I watched as the older boys snuck up behind Christian. As the teenagers were only a few feet away from my child they screamed real loud hoping for a fearful reaction. To my surprise, I watched my son turn around and take his sword and begin running full force towards the teenagers. Christian took his sword and ran them off saying, "You are not the police you can't yell at me." The older boys ran away from the sword as fast as they could in the opposite direction. It was hilarious, completely unexpected. What a sight to see. My small child chasing teenagers twice his size away from him. I couldn't help but laugh when my child fearlessly chased the "enemy" away.

My son was given wisdom beyond his years as he spoke out, "You are not the police you can't yell at me." What was he really saying? This is how I interpret it. His statement meant that others didn't have the authority to yell at him. He was saying, you don't have the authority to intimidate me, you haven't been given authority to mess with me. My son stood his ground and chased the "enemy" away. Christian had the victory and his confidence was not in himself, his confidence was in the sword that he carried. His confidence came from knowing who had the authority and who did not have authority. As he carried the sword, he was bold, courageous, and victorious! My child demonstrated what we as Gods children have been given, authority!

God spoke to me as I watched that happen. He was saying that just like Christian . . . We as Christians, have been given the same power and authority to use Gods word. The Bible is the sword of the spirit. (Ephesians 6:17) Our confidence is in the Lord not in our own ability. By speaking scriptures we take authority over the enemy, we make him run away. The enemy might try to yell or intimidate but as soon as we take the sword of the spirit, the word of God and say, "You have no authority to be here" we win because Jesus is the one with all power and authority, we stand our ground as Christians, we raise our voice, and we make the devil flee with the word of God. We have been given the victory in Christ Jesus.

> *". . . Be strong in the Lord and in his mighty power. Put on the full armor of God, so that you can take your stand against the devil's schemes. For our struggle is not against flesh and blood, but against the rulers, against the authorities, against the powers of this dark world and against the spiritual forces of evil in the heavenly realms. Therefore*

put on the full armor of God, so that when the day of evil comes, you may be able to stand your ground . . ." (Ephesians 6:10-13 NIV)

Just as the older kids tried to scare Christian so too does the enemy try to scare others. He lies, he deceives, he yells, he tries to intimidate. He tries to appear bigger than he is. Yet, if we as Christians will just pick up our swords which is the word of God and speak Gods words out . . . Then the enemy has no choice but to flee. We tell the enemy that he has no authority to speak to us and just as those teenagers ran so will he. With God on our side, we can take a stand declaring the truth of the gospel. What happens when we do that? The enemy must flee.

"Therefore put on the full armor of God, so that when the day of evil comes, you may be able to stand your ground, and after you have done everything, to stand. Stand firm then, with the belt of truth buckled around your waist, with the breastplate of righteousness in place, and with your feet fitted with the readiness that comes from the gospel of peace. In addition to all this, take up the shield of faith, with which you can extinguish all the flaming arrows of the evil one. Take the helmet of salvation and the sword of the Spirit, which is the word of God." (Ephesians 6:10-17 NIV)

God allowed me to witness in the natural what happens in the supernatural to us Christians when we use the word of God. We must learn to pick up our own swords and begin to stand upon Gods word just as those that have set great examples for us have. God, help me to memorize scriptures and use them as needed in my own life. Amen

"Be strong and courageous. Do not be afraid or terrified because of them, for the LORD your God goes with you; he will never leave you nor forsake you." (Deuteronomy 31:6)

Battle Won with Prayer

There are times when we must face an enemy as my son did. There are also times when the most courageous thing we can do is pray. Sometimes we simply need to pray for our enemies. Remember, our fight is not against people but against principalities.

> *"For we wrestle not against flesh and blood, but against principalities, against powers, against the rulers of the darkness of this world, against spiritual wickedness in high places."* (Ephesians 6:12 KJV)

The enemy is defeated and utterly destroyed by the word of God and by our prayers! The word of God is like a sword and it completely destroys the enemy. Here is another example of how God revealed this truth . . .

> *"You have heard that it was said, 'Love your neighbor and hate your enemy.' But I tell you, love your enemies and pray for those who persecute you, that you may be children of your Father in heaven.* (Matthew 5:43-45a)

While working at a previous job, I received a phone call from a very angry customer. She yelled at me so loud that my co-workers could hear her from the other side of the office. It was by far the worst phone call I ever received while working. I listened and responded in a very polite and calm manner. I could have easily walked away from that phone call with frustration. However, God placed a supernatural love in my heart for the caller. I felt as though she must have been verbally abused because no one would ever speak to a person like that unless they had experienced that themselves. During my lunch break, I prayed for her salvation and asked God to remove the "spirit of anger" she was dealing with. I asked God to save her soul, to heal her heart, and heal her emotions.

When I came back from my lunch break . . . The computers and phone lines were down. The power had been cut off. Maybe it was a coincidence but that person could no longer call the office. She no longer had the ability or power to yell or scream at me again. Almighty God heard my prayer. I find it very interesting that the "power of the air" had been cut off. (Ephesians 2:2)

That same night, I had a dream that I brutally killed a snake with a sword. The sword cut the snake into pieces. For someone who wouldn't hurt a fly. . . . it had to be a spiritual dream. The word of God is like a sword and it completely destroys the enemy! The snake in the dream represented a spiritual attack perhaps it was the "spirit of anger" that was cut off. The sword represents the word of God that utterly destroyed it. God allowed me to see what happens in the spirit realm with the power of our prayers.

> *"The word of God is alive and active, sharper than any double-edged sword"* (Hebrews 4:12 NIV)

The dream revealed the victory we obtain by the power of prayer. In the natural it didn't "feel" good to be yelled at. In the spirit God showed me I was victorious. Prayers are powerful, they cut off an attack from the enemy! The battle was not against the person it was against the spirit controlling that person. I guarantee that "snake" is gone forever. The victory did not come by returning anger for anger. No, the victory came by prayer, love, and by using the word of God. Love always wins!

I had the victory because I used the word of God. We are always victorious in Jesus name. We are called to love our neighbor. The battle was not won by getting angry at my neighbor the battle was won when I prayed for and loved my neighbor. When faced with an attack I simply spoke the word of God and won the fight! Thank you, Jesus!

Prayer

God forgive me for times when I have not used my sword, forgive me for allowing my my bible to collect dust. Help me to once again pick up the sword, the word of God, and use it correctly to help set captives free. God help me to walk in authority, to boldly speak the truth. I thank you that I can put on the full armor of God and fight, not in my own strength, but by the power of your word. Jesus you are victorious and so am I. As your child I have been given the victory. I will listen to your word and not what others say. Thank you, Jesus, for giving me the authority to stand on your word, I declare it, and the enemy must flee. Jesus, I thank you that the battle is already won. The enemy has already been defeated. I can be courageous in the fight as I declare your word. Thank you, Jesus that I am your child and I walk in victory because I walk with you. Amen.

Chapter 7

Under Our Feet

Vision of Angels on Assignment

ONE SUNDAY WHILE VISITING a church my husband had a vision of the supernatural realm during a time of worship. He said that the worship was building and building. A lot of people were up at the altar with their hands up. The music softened for a minute and the pastor of the church said he didn't want to interrupt what God was doing but he felt that a lady on the worship team had a prophetic song to share. She had a spontaneous song to sing that spoke about deliverance. She sang about Gods people being delivered from sickness, disease, fear, lust, anger, addictions and so on. Although a demon cannot possess a born again believer they can attach themselves to people through various sins or deception.

Suddenly, in the blink of an eye. My husband saw a very bright flash of light. The room was already light so he describes the light as though it was a flash of lightning on a sunny day. The room lit up. In an instant, several angelic angels came down to grab and snatch all the demons off of people. The angels removed all the demonic forces in the room. It happened so quickly that God allowed my husband to see it again in an instant replay.

In the blink of an eye, God sent Angels to remove all the demonic spirits off of people and set them free. Glory to God. There is power in prayer, there is power in worship, and there is power in the Name of Jesus. God sets people free from sin and deception. Sometimes God uses Angelic Angels as we pray to remove the dark forces around people. Amen!

Authority

God has given us the authority to tread on serpents, we have been given authority over all the power of the enemy, and nothing shall hurt us. Scripture tells us that we have the authority to tread on serpents. God has given us authority over all the power of the enemy! (Luke 10:19)

> *"Behold, I have given you authority to tread on serpents and scorpions, and over all the power of the enemy, and nothing shall hurt you." (Luke 10:19 ESV)*

"And the great dragon was thrown down, that ancient serpent, who is called the devil and satan, the deceiver of the whole world—he was thrown down to the earth...."

Revelation 12:9 ESV

According to scripture, a serpent is mentioned as a deceiver, the devil. A snake is something demonic and it's meant to be under our feet. As believers in Christ, God has given us the power to tread on serpents. The definition for tread is to set down a foot in walking, to press, to crush, and to destroy. To take a stand and say no devil, no devil, no, no, no. He is under our feet, we have authority over him. The words we say are powerful. We have the ability to command the enemy to leave as we speak or sing songs of deliverance. As believers we have been given power over the enemy and power over sin by the blood of Jesus. Unfortunately the same cannot be said for the unbeliever.

Shutting the Mouth of the Enemy

Recently the Holy Spirit reminded me of a time where he had taken me on a journey to a third world country. This was a vision given by Jesus to reveal a battle in the spirit realm. As believers in Christ Jesus we have power and authority over the enemy. However, those that do not believe in Jesus are in serious danger. The enemy deceives the unbeliever and those living under spiritual deception. It is our job as believers to pray for them. Without our prayers and without Jesus, they are helpless.

By the supernatural power of the Holy Spirit, I traveled to a desert-like environment land, dry and blistering hot. It was in the middle of nowhere. There wasn't any vegetation for miles on end, no trees, no shelter, and no area to find shade. It was dry and barren with an empty atmosphere. The only thing in sight for miles around was one area with something that looked like a pergola. Four wooden columns or posts coming up from the ground with a few beams connecting across the top. There was no roof, it was just an open area with no shelter.

The largest snake you can imagine was on top of the wooden poles. The snake was thick and twisted, it wrapped around the top of the wooden structure many times. Although the snake had twisted around the pieces of wood numerous times. Without exaggerating, the snake appeared to be at least thirty feet long. It was massive. I went over to the snake, without fear, and I took both of my hands to shut its mouth. The head of the snake was large.

As soon as I shut the snake's mouth, I could see a person standing near the snake. It was the middle of the day and they appeared as having dark hair, I don't recall if it was a male or female. While holding the mouth of the snake shut I yelled out to the person saying, "Watch out for its tale" I knew the snake could no longer speak because I had shut its mouth. However, its tail was so huge that it could still wrap around and kill the person standing around it.

As I warned about the snake's tail, I knew there was a double meaning in that warning. I was warning them about the "tale" as in the lies, the deception. I was warning someone to stop listening to the twisted lies of the devil and see that to be under its tale of deception was a dangerous place to be. Even when the voice of the enemy is stopped or shut, the lies that someone had once believed can still be deadly. If the "tale" continued on it could constrict or try to squeeze the life out of someone completely. Only by walking away from the lies and deception would they be safe. As soon as I yelled out the warning to watch out for the tail of deception, I woke up.

I have been given authority by God to break the power of the enemy in someone's life. God had me to speak truth over a spiritual battle that person was dealing with. I shut the voice of the enemy and gave a warning to someone of an attack. Someone under enemy deception needed a believer to stand in prayer and come against the power of the enemy. Snakes belong under our feet, however, that person had allowed the enemy to be raised up to a place it did not belong in their life, in a place above their head. It was a demonic spirit that needed to be taken down in prayer. The enemy voice needed to be silenced and brought down under foot, crushed, and destroyed.

I pray the truth of Jesus penetrates that region as the voice of the enemy is shut. I pray that areas of lies of deception are seen for what they are. May Jesus bring freedom to those who are living under any form of deception. We have been given the power and authority to tread on serpents, and over all the power of the enemy, and nothing shall hurt us that believe in Jesus Christ, The Lord.

> *"Behold, I have given you authority to tread on serpents and scorpions, and over all the power of the enemy, and nothing shall hurt you." (Luke 10:19 ESV)*

Breaking Deception

Jesus wants His believers to pray to set others free! I know that vision is a dramatic illustration of the spiritual battle, but God used it to show the seriousness of it. Many people are standing in a dangerous place, a place that only Jesus can set them free from. Souls are in danger of going to hell if they do not cry out to Jesus for salvation, forgiveness, and mercy. There is no shelter, no roof, no covering, no protection, when a person is living under deception. The environment in that place is empty, dry, and barren.

Deception is more than just being lied to, that word also implies having a false idea or belief. May God open the eyes of those who are walking in ignorance, false beliefs, and false ideas. May those who are under any form of deception see that Jesus is the only way to freedom. Freedom is found in Christ Jesus alone. There is only one place to find a safe shelter. A shelter of protection from the enemy can only be found in Jesus.

> "So if the son sets you free, you will be free indeed." (John 8:36 NIV)

Jesus, the Only Way

Truth tells us that Jesus is the only way to the Father. Jesus is the only way to God. Jesus answered, *"I am the way and the truth and the life. No one comes to the Father except through me."* John 14:6 Jesus is the truth. Truth says there is only one way to God and that way is Jesus.

Those who are unsure about Jesus often say it doesn't make sense that a good God would only allow only one way to Him. Although it is a good question it is not the right question. The question that should be asked is, "How can a Holy God allow people like us to even have one way to Him?" We are so blessed to even be allowed to have a relationship with Jesus.

Imagine a person being trapped in a room of fire with no windows and only one door. That person would be very grateful to find that one and only door of escape. They would not complain that there was only one door. No, they would be very grateful they found the one door to safety. They would be very thankful that they had access to the one and only door of escape. That door would save their soul from torment. Only Jesus can save a person's soul from eternal suffering. That door is Jesus. He is the only way to God our Father. I am thankful for that door!

> *"Then said Jesus unto them again, verily, verily, I say unto you, I am the door of the sheep."* (John 10:7 KJV)

Salvation for those who trust in Jesus

Only those that trust in Jesus will be saved. Jesus is the door. The only way to God, and the only way to be safe from destruction. Remember the story of Noah's Ark? Noah's ark was an Old Testament picture of how we as Christians are saved from God's wrath and judgment. When we are safely found in Christ Jesus we escape judgment. All other paths lead to destruction.

God saved Noah and his family because they trusted God. There came a time when the door of God's mercy shut, the ark closed, people were screaming outside, unable to be saved. The flood destroyed. Yet, God saved Noah's family because they trusted in him. They were kept safe and secure in God. The only way to be saved today is also to enter by the door. Jesus is that door. Jesus is the one and only way to escape the judgment of God.

All those that call on the name of the Lord Jesus will be saved. Call on his name because one day the door will be shut. We only have so many years on earth. Will you enter God's kingdom by way of Jesus, the door? Or will you be stuck outside screaming as in the days of Noah? Wishing you trusted Jesus while you still had the chance? I'm thankful I trust him and I can share Jesus with others who need to trust him as well. I am glad to be in the family of God.

Believing God

What are you believing God for? Strength in the battle? The salvation of souls? The salvation of a family member? The salvation of a people group? To help set others free from deception? To share the gospel truth with boldness and power? To share Jesus with your friends? To be a light in the darkness? To be a witness at work? To free others from false beliefs? To free others from addictions? To heal others by the power of the Holy Spirit? Jesus offers freedom to all who call on His name. Jesus sets people free and yes He will use you to free others as you believe in Him. Remember, the enemy is under your feet. You have been given spiritual authority to speak the word of God and break the power of the enemy in Jesus Name.

Prayer

Thank you, Jesus, the enemy is under my feet. I declare as it says in Psalm 91 that shelter is found only in the Lord Almighty. Jesus is the only way and he is the door. I bind the spirit of deception and pray that you Jesus will open the eyes of those living under any form of it. Thank you, Jesus, for setting people free. Jesus, you have all power and all authority and you Lord Jesus are the most high. Anything that is not of you and anything that would try to raise itself up to a place that it does not belong would be cast down and trampled underfoot. Jesus, thank you for rescuing those that call on your name. Salvation and deliverance can only be found in you, Lord Jesus. Thank you, Jesus, for salvation. Thank you for deliverance from the enemy. Help us to worship you Jesus and thank you for sending Angels from heaven to remove anything that is not of you. In Jesus name, I pray. Amen.

Chapter 8

Fragrance of the Holy Spirit

Supernatural Encounter: The Aroma of Christ

TODAY, I SET ASIDE time with Jesus, I listened to some bible teachings and was thinking about the goodness of God. Suddenly, I felt a wave of the Holy Spirit touching my heart and I could smell a sweet smelling fragrance. The aroma was like flowers, it reminded me of anointing oil. I sensed the presence of God and I could smell the anointing of the Holy Spirit. The fragrance of the Holy Spirit was in my house. I could actually smell the aroma of Christ in my living room. I did not have any flowers in my home or any perfume around me. I was alone with the Holy Spirit. The Holy Spirit touched my heart while I experienced the fragrance of God and felt His presence at the same time. The fragrance of His presence is so sweet.

I'm thankful that Gods presence is available to us. He is found in the secret place of prayer. He is found in quiet times, in times at home, when you are alone, in times when no one else is looking. God is found in a daily relationship with Him. He is found in reading His word, He is found in a devotional book, He is found in your private times of worship. He is with you. As you spend time with Him a supernatural encounter can happen during a quiet time when it is just you and Jesus.

> *"But thanks be to God, who always leads us in triumph in Christ, and through us spreads and makes evident everywhere the sweet fragrance of the knowledge of Him." (2 Corinthians 2:14 AMP)*

The Fragrance of the Knowledge of Christ

Scripture teaches that there is a fragrance of the knowledge of Christ. As we seek to know Him, we can actually experience the aroma of Christ.

> *"Therefore become imitators of God [copy Him and follow His example], as well-beloved children [imitate their father]; and walk continually in love [that is, value one another—practice empathy and compassion, unselfishly seeking the best for others], just as Christ also loved you and gave Himself up for us, an offering and sacrifice to God [slain for you, so that it became] a sweet fragrance."*
>
> *Ephesians 5:1-2 AMP*

But thanks be to God, who always leads us in triumph in Christ, and manifests through us the sweet aroma of the knowledge of him in every place. 2 Corinthians 2:14 NASB

Imitate Christ

Jesus did many things, Jesus taught, Jesus prayed, Jesus healed people, Jesus fed people. Whatever Jesus was doing he was always serving people. He is full of kindness and compassion. Everywhere Jesus went he helped the people around him. That is what we are all called to do, to serve others. Whether it's from the platform, leading people in worship, or teaching, feeding people, giving a cold cup of water, praying for people, listening to someone in need, no matter how we serve, we wake up every day and ask, "How can we serve you, God?" We say, "How can we bless your people today?" God will provide divine appointments as you look to bless others around you.

God asks that we become imitators of Christ and that we walk in love for each other. Jesus loved us and gave himself up for us as an offering and sacrifice to God and it became a sweet fragrance. God asks that we practice empathy and compassion and seek the best for others. As children of God, we can imitate our Father and be willing to sacrifice unselfishly and seek the best for others. What aroma is your life producing before God? Do you smell like the world? Or is there an aroma of Christ in your life?

"For we are a fragrance of Christ to God among those who are being saved and among those who are perishing;"

2 Corinthians 2:15 NASB

Carrying His Presence

As believers, we carry the presence of God. He is with us. In God's presence, healings can occur. As believers, we are carriers of God's presence and his presence heals people. God's presence is especially important when praying for the unbeliever. God wants us, as believers, to introduce unbelievers to his presence. They can feel his presence as we pray for them. Sometimes a person may feel warmth or power as the Holy Spirit flows through a believer. The most important thing is for them to feel God's heart of compassion and his love for them. We carry the presence of God everywhere we go. The presence and the glory of God is a very powerful thing that removes all fear and anxiety. In His presence, all fear is gone! As we carry God's presence we share the aroma of Christ and his presence is what heals people.

FRAGRANCE OF THE HOLY SPIRIT

"For we are a fragrance of Christ to God among those who are being saved and among those who are perishing;" (2 Corinthians 2:15 NASB)

Releasing the Kingdom of God

Let me share an example. Last summer I took an art class at a local college. It was a six-hour class. During our first break, one of the students came up to me.

She said, "I have anxiety, is it ok if we talk for a little while? I just need to talk it out, and I will feel better." I replied, "Sure" and listened for a few minutes. Then, I asked if I could pray for her. She agreed. I prayed that she would feel God's presence. Then, I commanded the anxiety to leave in Jesus Name. I thanked the Holy Spirit for touching her life and for letting her feel the peace of God.

After I prayed, she thanked me and said, "Wow, I really do feel better. I feel peace" I could tell she was surprised that the prayer worked but she could not deny the fact that she felt peace. As born again Christians, we carry God's presence and for someone who does not believe, we are able to let them feel His presence simply by praying for them. When praying for an unbeliever, we as Christians have the power to release the kingdom of God here on earth.

How do you share Jesus?

What is your gift? What gift has God given you to bless his people with? Seek him for wisdom, stay in connection with him, trust him every day, spend time resting in his presence, Trust God will use you for the things he has called you to. The days and times are in his hands. Communicate with Jesus every day in prayer and ask him for help to reach others around you. Share the fragrance of the knowledge of Christ everywhere you go.

The Perfect Gift

Consider this analogy.... One of the best purchases I've ever made was a kitchen blender. I enjoy making healthy and delicious fruit smoothies for myself and my family. For a while, I was making smoothies every day. The fruit smoothies not only taste good they also look amazing. I have fun blending different fruit and watching as the smoothies are created. They are rich in color and beautiful to look at. My blender comes with a medium and large cup that I can use depending on the amount of fruit I want to blend.

One Christmas, my son gave me the perfect gift. It was a small cup to fit my blender! It was the perfect size to make an individual smoothie, just for me. My son and my husband both watched as I opened that gift and was so very excited to receive such a treasure. I thought to myself, "my son really knows what I like, that was the perfect gift, I love it so much, and I will use it often."

A few months later, my family was out shopping. I found the blenders and walked over to appreciate them. I located my blender with the various size cups. I noticed that the individual cup sizes were not for sale at that particular store. I showed them to my son and thanked him again for the gift he had given me. At that time, my son smiled and said, "Mom, I didn't actually buy you the small cup for your blender" I was shocked and asked him to explain. He told me that when I originally purchased the blender that it came with three sizes, small, medium, and large. However, I had only used the larger sizes and had left the small cup in the original box it came in. I had forgotten I had it. He gave me a gift I already had. I laughed at his creativity. He didn't spend any money and yet he gave me the perfect gift, one I already had. I also shook my head as I realized I had truly forgotten what I had already been given.

My family watched as I got so excited about receiving a treasure that I already had. You see, I've got the Holy Spirit living on the inside of me, the treasure of God is on the inside of me already. I can't forget to use what God has already given me. The moment I got saved there was treasure deposited on the inside of me. The Holy Spirit empowers each of us to do and be what we cannot do in our own ability or strength. You are equipped to follow the calling of God for your life and to produce good fruit by the power of the Holy Spirit.

The Holy Spirit gives each of us various gifts to use. Sometimes we can be so focused on using a few of the gifts he has given that we could actually forget to use other gifts he has provided us with. Use your gifts, all of them, to help the world around you. Try not to forget the gifts he has already provided you with!

For example, if Jesus gave me three gifts such as teaching, service, and intercession. I should use all three gifts. For a while I may have only used my gifts of teaching and service however I had forgotten about the gift of intercession. One day that gift reappears and guess what? I had it all along. You give God glory by using all the gifts he has given you to produce sweet-smelling fruit for His kingdom.

Pray and Use Your Gifts

1 Peter 4:10 says " *Each of you should use whatever gift you have received to serve others, as faithful stewards of God's grace in its various forms." (1 Peter 4:10 NIV)*

What gifts has God given you? There are so many ways to share Jesus with the world around you. Open up your gifts and share them with the world around you.

Walk in the Anointing

> *"As for you, the anointing you received from him remains in you, and you do not need anyone to teach you. But as his anointing teaches you about all things and as that anointing is real, not counterfeit—just as it has taught you, remain in him."* 1 John 2:27 NIV

We can walk in the anointing when we share the fragrance of the knowledge of Christ with others. As children of God, we represent him, and we are called to care for those around us with a heart of compassion. For we are a fragrance of Christ to those around us. (2 Corinthians 2:15) What gifts has God placed inside you. Are you walking in all the gifts he has provided you with, or have you forgotten to use some of them as I did?

- Administration
- Apostleship
- Craftsmanship
- Discernment
- Evangelism
- Exhortation
- Faith
- Giving
- Healing
- Helps
- Hospitality
- Intercession
- Words of knowledge
- Leadership
- Mercy
- Miracles
- Pastor/Shepherd
- Prophecy
- Service
- Teaching
- Tongues
- Word of Wisdom

Victory, A Place of Fragrance

Keep walking with God and you will experience the "sweet smell of victory" the fragrance of Christ. The word "Jericho" is described as a "place of fragrance" Joshua entered Jericho, the Promised Land and the walls surrounding the city were destroyed. (Joshua 6) He enjoyed the sweet smell of victory. Is there a wall standing in your way? Is there anything keeping you from doing what God has called you to do? Is there anything keeping you, or someone you know, from entering into the promises of God. God wants us to enter a land of plenty.

God wants us to experience the fragrance of a life lived in him. In the natural, you may not be able to move a wall or obstacle, but supernaturally all things are possible. Your prayers can move mountains and walls! Do not fear, the wall of fear and anxiety must leave in Jesus name. There is peace in the presence of God. Whatever wall you are facing, it will come down by the power of prayer. Walls are coming down in Jesus name. Amen.

Thank God, he always leads us in triumph in Christ Jesus. (2 Corinthians 2:14) We are always triumphant in Christ. Any walls that have hindered you, or the people you know, from walking in the calling God has for you, those walls will crumble and fall at the name of Jesus. Nothing can stand in God's way. If God has promised you something, keep believing him for it. No matter what obstacle you may be facing, you can hold onto the promises of God for your life. Listen to what God says and follow His instructions to victory. Walk in the things God has planned for your life. What has God promised you? What has he called you to? Hold onto his promises.

Keep walking with God

I thank God that we can still experience the miraculous but we also need to be faithful in our daily routine. Joshua heard the voice of God and he obeyed the instructions God gave him for victory. God shows up when we invite him into our daily lives. God is looking to partner with us, and he needs partners who will represent him well. God needs faithful servants who will pray when no one else is looking, who will keep their word when no one is looking. He is looking for servants who will guard their heart in the things they say, watch, and hear. He wants to partner with his children, but we need to do our part in representing him well. We need to be listening for his voice each day and looking to obey him in the things he says. He is looking for faithful stewards. When God speaks we need to follow the instruction he gives. It doesn't matter what anyone else but God says. God's opinion is the only opinion that really matters. What did God say? Declare what God says. You have the sweet smell of victory in Christ Jesus. It is his will that you prosper and be in good health even as your soul prospers. (3 John 1:2)

"He called you to be partners with his Son Jesus Christ our Lord"

1 Corinthians 1:9b Gods Word Translation

Keep believing God. Your mountain(s) will move. Remain faithful in what he has called you to each day. Believe him for big things and obey him in the smallest of things. Believe him for miraculous things, dream big because God has no limit to what he can do for you and through you. Believe him for things you can't do on your own, that way he will always get the glory, it's all about him. He is just waiting for people who will trust him and pray in agreement with him and his Word. He is looking for vessels he can flow through.

God will use your unique gifts to further his kingdom. Jesus served those around him and loved them. He served people and we are to imitate Jesus as sons and daughters of God Almighty. Our lives can be fragrant to God as we love and serve those around us. Keep on marching with Jesus! Let us not become weary in well doing. Don't give up. Expect Gods supernatural provision as you walk in His ways.

Dreams Given by God

Recently, God spoke to me in a dream. I have a friend and prayer partner who I have been meeting with for the past several weeks. In the dream, my friend left her phone at my house. She had been without her phone for several days before I noticed she had forgotten it. I picked her phone up to see if she had missed any messages or if she had missed any calls. She had not missed a message or a call during that time. While holding her phone, I scrolled through it and noticed she had a video that she had taken at another friend's house. I thought to myself, "That house is on this phone because she is called to pray for it." I put her phone down and prepared to give it back to her.

The second part of the dream, I was standing outside in the sun. Someone came up to me and asked what day I was planning to go on vacation. This time I looked at my own phone and surprisingly the calendar that was previously on my phone was missing. I was unable to look at my calendar. I first needed to contact someone before I could get the days and times.

Dream Interpretation

Prayer warriors, friends of God. Only you can answer the call of God on your life. Only you can walk in the anointing he has placed on your life. No one else can do that for you. A phone is symbolic of our connection with God. Prayer is talking to God. If my phone is not directly connected to a power source it is worthless. The same is true in our lives. Every day we must daily connect with God in prayer. The only power source is Jesus. Daily, we must be plugged into the source and connect with God.

We cannot allow a few days to pass without getting a message from Gods Word or without hearing His voice. We should not allow a few days to pass without connecting in prayer. We are all called to pray for others and don't forget that. God puts certain people in your life so that you can reach them. No one else can pick up your calling to intercede as you can. Sure, others may be able to agree in prayer with you. Yet, ultimately the call on your life to reach the people in your own area of influence belongs to you and no one else.

Others may be able to recognize a portion of what God is calling you to. They may be able to sense the anointing on your life. They may be able to pick up on or have a glimpse into some of the things God has for your life. However, the calling God has for you, is for you specifically and no one else. Only you can do what God called you to. Your prayers matter to God. Others can agree in prayer but you are ultimately responsible to pray for the things He puts on your heart.

For myself, I had my personal phone with me, I knew my calling and I was walking in connection with the Lord. I am walking in the light. However, I must rely on God and rest in him. I must slow down and rest in Jesus and spend more time with him. I was unable to know the days or times without first seeking help from God. The timing is not in my hands the timing is God's hands. I need to trust his timing. I can rest knowing that his timing is perfect. He is the one in charge of my days. He is the one who knows the plans he has prepared for me. God has a plan for my life and I just need to rest in him and trust him for the timing. Amen!

Connect with God daily, receive messages from his word, and listen to his voice. Use your gifting as only you can. My friend has the gift of intercession, she is called to pray for the burdens God puts on her heart.

Encountering God during sleep

God often speaks to his people while they sleep to keep them from pride. If we are resting, or sleeping, then God gets full credit for what he chooses to reveal to us. We don't do any of the work. It is by God's grace, and not by our works. It is truly by the leading of the Holy Spirit and not by striving to solve things in our own mind. We don't obtain victories by our own works but only by his grace. We can rest in him and know that battle belongs to the Lord. Supernatural dreams and wisdom come from God.

The Bible speaks about this in Job 33:14-16

> *"Indeed God speaks once, Or twice, yet no one notices it. "In a dream, a vision of the night, when sound sleep falls on men, while they slumber in their beds. Then He opens the ears of men and seals their instruction." (Job 33:14-16 NASB)*

The Lord visits people during the night and gives them instructions while they sleep. God speaks, and he gets all the glory.

> *"I will praise the Lord, who counsels me; even at night my heart instructs me."*
>
> *Psalm 16:7 NIV*

Prayer

Lord Jesus help me to do what you want me to do. Let my life be a fragrant aroma to you. Acceptable in your sight. Instruct me, speak to my heart, and lead me each day. Help me to serve others with the gifts you have given me, and may it be a fragrant offering to you, Jesus. Help me to bear fruit for your kingdom. Amen

Chapter 9

Power of the Holy Spirit

WHEN DIVINE ENCOUNTERS ARE given, they produce change. The Holy Bible gives numerous accounts of supernatural occurrences. Each time someone encounters God, Jesus, or the Holy Spirit they are immediately changed. The book of Acts chapter 2 gives an account of the disciples hiding in the upper room. They were scared, they were hiding. One moment they were totally afraid. The Jews were being persecuted, Jesus had gone to the cross, and they were frightened. Then they had an encounter with the Holy Spirit that immediately transformed their lives.

Acts 2: 1-4 New International Version (NIV)

The Holy Spirit at Pentecost

"When the day of Pentecost came, they were all together in one place. Suddenly a sound like the blowing of a violent wind came from heaven and filled the whole house where they were sitting. They saw what seemed to be tongues of fire that separated and came to rest on each of them. All of them were filled with the Holy Spirit and began to speak in other tongues[a] as the Spirit enabled them."

The same Peter who denied Jesus to a little girl, when Jesus was arrested, was transformed into a bold, powerful, preacher of the gospel. When the Holy Spirit came into the room, all the disciples became bold. They were filled with power that they didn't have before. They had faith in God, and they believed in Him, yet they were still scared and in hiding. Once they had an encounter with the Holy Spirit, they didn't care about their own lives anymore. Everything changed, hiding was no longer an option. They dedicated their lives to the work of the kingdom from that day forward.

A Christian who has not received power by the Holy Spirit will most likely hide and not share the gospel. Do you know anyone like that? After the disciples were filled with the Holy Spirit, they shared the gospel effectively.

Talk about a transformation! After they received the Holy Spirit, they became bold, they shared the salvation message of Jesus, they set people free from unbelief, they started churches, and Peter decided to share the gospel with all people groups, not only the Jewish people. The Holy Spirit did the work through his willing vessels to build the church.

Acts 2:7-13 NIV
"Utterly amazed, they asked: "Aren't all these who are speaking Galileans? Then how is it that each of us hears them in our native language . . . Amazed and perplexed, they asked one another, "What does this mean? Some, however, made fun of them and said, "They have had too much wine."

The Holy Spirit has a way of revealing what is in a person's heart. Notice that as soon as the Holy Spirit arrived some people began to make fun of the disciples. Don't be surprised when supernatural events happen in your life and others begin to "make fun" in verse thirteen we see that some people made fun of the Holy Spirits work because they did not understand it. They were asking each other, "What does this mean?" They were perplexed. The supernatural is difficult to understand in the natural. Oftentimes the work of the Holy Spirit does not make sense to the human mind. They had to hear the word first. Faith comes by hearing the word. Peter had to explain before they could understand. As they listened to the gospel they began to believe.

We see from the scriptures that new believers were baptized and raised to new life. The baptism is where they had freedom from sin. Their sin had to die, it had to be buried in water, and they were raised up into new life, they became a new creation, and they were born again. Peter shares the gospel and three thousand people got saved that very day. Everyone that accepted the message got baptized into a new life with Christ!

Peter Addresses the Crowd

Acts 2:14-40
"Then Peter stood up with the Eleven, raised his voice and addressed the crowd: "Fellow Jews and all of you who live in Jerusalem, let me explain this to you; listen carefully to what I say. These people are not drunk, as you suppose. It's only nine in the morning! No, this is what was spoken by the prophet Joel:"

Stand on the Word of God

Peter stood up, he took a stand. Peter shared his faith and he raised his voice. As followers of Christ, we will face opposition. When Peter heard the crowd make fun of the believers, he decided to take a stand. Peter stood up. Do we stand up and face opposition when it comes our way? The first thing Peter needed to do was stand. He stood his ground and then he shared the gospel message in response to the opposition questioning. He spoke the word of God. Peter was bold, he raised his voice. He began sharing the message by saying, this is what "God says" He spoke with authority from the word of God.

"'In the last days, God says, I will pour out my Spirit on all people. Your sons and daughters will prophesy, your young men will see visions, your old men will dream dreams. Even on my servants, both men, and women, I will pour out my Spirit in those days, and they will prophesy . . ."

Peter shared scripture and explained the work of the Holy Spirit. God was pouring out His spirit. They were experiencing that outpouring. God pours out his Spirit on his servants, God's children. Peter shares the entire salvation message with those that were questioning the Holy Spirit and they listened. Peter continues. . . .

"Fellow Israelites listen to this: Jesus of Nazareth was a man accredited by God to you by miracles, wonders, and signs, which God did among you through him, as you yourselves know. This man was handed over to you by God's deliberate plan and foreknowledge; and you, with the help of wicked men, put him to death by nailing him to the cross. But God raised him from the dead, freeing him from the agony of death because it was impossible for death to keep its hold on him. David said about him:"

Peter begins speaking and basically says listen up, let me tell you about Jesus. His opening words are "Listen to this" He continues. Jesus did miracles, signs, and wonders by the power of God. Wicked men put him to death. Jesus was crucified but he was raised from the dead. Jesus has power over death and the grave. Death has no hold on him. God raised Jesus to life, and they were witnesses of it.

"Therefore let all Israel be assured of this: God has made this Jesus, whom you crucified, both Lord and Messiah." When the people heard this, they were cut to the heart and said to Peter and the other apostles, *"Brothers, what shall we do?"*

The moment they realized that Jesus is Lord and Messiah it pierced their heart. That was the convicting power of the Holy Spirit. When the servants of God worked together with the Holy Spirit it resulted in repentance and true salvation for others. Their response was what can we do? They realized how wrong they had been. They knew something needed to be done. How could they be forgiven?

"Peter replied, *"Repent and be baptized, every one of you, in the name of Jesus Christ for the forgiveness of your sins. And you will receive the gift of the Holy Spirit. The promise is for you and your children and for all who are far off—for all whom the Lord our God will call."*

With many other words, he warned them; and he pleaded with them, "Save yourselves from this corrupt generation." Those who accepted his message were baptized, and about three thousand were added to their number that day."

What was the outcome of this encounter with the Holy Spirit? Those that were making fun of the Holy Spirit were cut to the heart. They came to the realization that they desperately needed Jesus. They had a turning point, they repented for their unbelief. They got baptized for the forgiveness of their sins. They called on the name of the Lord.

And everyone who calls on the name of the Lord will be saved.

Power to Share the Gospel

Disciples were given the power to share the good news. Disciples were transformed from fearfully hiding to being bold and courageous in faith. They expand the kingdom. Thousands of people responded to the salvation message. Thousands of people believed. Thousands of people got baptized. The Holy Spirit did not just fill the disciples to give them a few Holy Ghost goose bumps. They didn't experience the power of the Holy Spirit to keep it to themselves. No, they powerfully shared Jesus with others.

Their encounter with the Holy Spirit brought about immediate changes. They were never the same again. The disciple's lives were transformed by Jesus, and they were given the Holy Spirits power to share the gospel with others. As they shared the gospel three thousand lives were changed in just one day and more lives would be changed in the days following. What an encounter that was! Thank you, Jesus!

Gods' power is best found at our weakest moments. I'm sure the disciples were heartbroken after Jesus was crucified. They were hiding and surely they were discouraged. People were dying and being persecuted just for following Jesus. They didn't have the strength to share the gospel at that time. The disciples were just hoping to stay alive. Life was difficult, I'm sure they were at the point of questioning their beliefs. Jesus was gone. They didn't have direction on what to do next. They felt alone, frightened, and scared. Yet, 2 Corinthians 12:9 declares "My grace is sufficient for you, for my power is made perfect in weakness." Therefore I will boast all the more gladly about my weaknesses, so that Christ's power may rest on me.

They received the Holy Spirit when they felt alone. Christ's power rest upon them. They exchanged their weakness for Christ's power. God has given his servants the power of the Holy Spirit to share the good news with others! Every believer can advance the kingdom and share the gospel. I've got some good news to share.

Prayer

Thank you, God, I can stand on your word. Thank you, God, for pouring out your Holy Spirit on all people. Thank you, Father God, that your sons and daughters will prophesy, young men, will see visions and old men will dream dreams. Thank you for pouring out your Spirit on your servants both men and women. Jesus, thank you for filling me with your Holy Spirit. Thank you for the opportunity to share the good news with others. Amen

Chapter 10

A Life Transformed

WHEN JESUS SHOWS UP lives are transformed. Jesus transforms. Love transforms. One of the most powerful examples of a life transformed in the Bible was that of Saul. God transformed the life of Saul an unbeliever who would persecute and kill Christians into a new person whom he called Paul. Paul became a missionary who shared the gospel with many people groups. Paul wrote half of the New Testament. Gods' wisdom guided Paul in his writing and in everything he did. The more you read Paul's writings the more you see his immense spirit of gratitude. Paul was an amazing man of God and yet humble at the same time. He never forgot what God did to change his life, he was grateful for it.

When Saul was on the road to Damascus, he was on his way to persecute the church. Jesus shows up, reveals himself to Saul, and is full of mercy towards him. Jesus asks Saul why he was persecuting Him. Saul is blinded (temporarily) and has a moment with God where he comes to the realization of who Jesus really is. He makes peace with God and acknowledges Jesus as the Messiah.

Before Saul's encounter with God, he was persecuting Christians, after his encounter with God, his life was transformed. Paul's life transformed so much so that God gave him a completely new name, a new identity, Paul had become an entirely different person. When someone is born again, they become new. What a beautiful example of a life transformed by God. When God shows up in a person life, they are completely different. Such Amazing Grace!

Transformed into a New Person

Those that are not saved are like Saul, blind unable to see. Thank God for his amazing grace! He opens the eyes of the blind, He changes a person and makes them completely new. Only God can save a soul that once was lost and make them new. How precious is that grace indeed. God calls us believers to share that good news with those walking in blindness.

What was the outcome of Saul's encounter with God? He became a new person who shared the message of Christ Jesus with everyone he knew. He furthered the kingdom of God. When a person gets a true revelation of who Christ really is then they are forever changed. The desire to evangelize to those around and to share the truth of gospel intensifies.

We are all called to be ministers to those around us, to live in a way that is noticeably different. We are called to be a light to the world. We will never influence the world by trying to be like it. We are to stand out and to be different.

Shine your Light

"You are the light of the world. A town built on a hill cannot be hidden. Neither do people light a lamp and put it under a bowl, instead, they put it on its stand, and it gives light to everyone in the house. In the same way, let your light shine before others, that they may see your good deeds and glorify your Father in heaven."

Matthew 5:14-16 NIV

God wants us to shine the light of Jesus all around, everywhere we go. Are you sharing Jesus with people you meet? Are you ministering everywhere you go?

"Don't you have a saying? You say, it's still four months until harvest time. But I tell you, open your eyes! Look at the fields! They are ripe for harvest right now." John 4:35

Open your eyes, look at the fields. They are ripe for harvest.

We don't have the same story as Saul. However, Jesus tells us to open our eyes, he wants us to plant or share His word with people around us, to family, to our workplace, to the community, and beyond. Jesus has set us free, we are no longer blind because of unbelief, but are we looking at the fields? When we see Jesus for who he really is, then we can't help but share the good news with others! When our eyes are open, we see those in need around us. When Jesus transforms a life, it is so other lives will be transformed too. Share your testimony with others, walk in love and be an example to those around you.

Look at the fields

An encounter with Jesus changes everything! Look at the fields. Where is your field? What does your field look like? Just think if you decide to pray for a different person every day. Just pray for one person a day. What would happen? A year later you have sown 365 prayers into 365 lives. Faithfulness in small things adds up to much in Gods sight. Just imagine if a family of three people reached out to one person a day they would make an impact in a year of more than one thousand lives!

A Life of Prayer

Another example we can take from the life of Paul is that he prayed in the Holy Spirit more than anyone he knew. Paul urged believers in Christ to continually pray without ceasing. It is Gods will that we give thanks in all circumstances and continue to pray without stopping,

"Pray without ceasing. In everything give thanks: for this is the will

of God in Christ Jesus concerning you"

1 Thessalonians 5:17:18 KJV

Paul lived a life of prayer!

> *"I thank God that I speak in tongues more than all of you. But in the church, I would rather speak five intelligible words to instruct others than ten thousand words in a tongue" (1 Corinthians 14:18)*

When we don't know how to pray we can ask God for wisdom on how best to pray. "If any of you lacks wisdom, he should ask God, who gives generously to all without finding fault, and it will be given to him" (James 1:5) God generously gives wisdom to those that ask for it. When God imparts wisdom to us, we can rest assured that he knows what he is talking about. Instead of praying with uncertainty, we seek his wisdom. We can also pray in the Holy Spirit and allow the Spirit to intercede through us. (Romans 8:26–27)

The Holy Spirit Intercedes

"In the same way the Spirit also helps our weakness; for we do not know how to pray as we should, but the Spirit Himself intercedes for us with groanings too deep for words; and He who searches the hearts knows what the mind of the Spirit is, because He intercedes for the saints according to the will of God." (Romans 8:26-27 NASB)

Jesus can release prayer plans and strategies straight from heaven. If we get instruction from Jesus on how to pray, we will see results as our prayers agree with the very heart of God. When we get a revelation of His heart, we can pray the very heart of Jesus. Jesus is the best prayer partner to have. When Jesus agrees with your prayers you will surely see the power of prayer in agreement with Him.

The Voice of the Holy Spirit

Tune into the voice of the Holy Spirit, hear from heaven and line your prayers up with his prayers and will, releasing the supernatural into the natural. Seek to find prayer plans straight from heaven. Open your ears to hear what God is saying and allow him to lead you. With wisdom imparted from Jesus, our prayers become strategic. Pray strategically in him. He always listens to his children.

"Let us draw near to God with a sincere heart and with full assurance of faith"

Hebrews 10:22a NIV

Jesus intercedes for us and since he is our example, we should intercede for others too. (Romans 8:34) Jesus prays all the time for us, he knows exactly how to pray. He knows what we need before we need it, he knows what we think before we think it. He knows exactly what everyone needs. When we don't know what to pray for or how to pray, we can pray in the Holy Spirit. We are called to intercede for others. We continue to pray until they experience a breakthrough. Your prayers matter, your faithful prayers make a difference. Keep believing!

He Hears Your Cry

I remember when I heard the cry of a child in my neighborhood. Jesus asked me to stop and help him. A child was locked out of his own home. He couldn't find his key and was beginning to feel fear and anxiety. I reassured him everything would be alright. Just then, I noticed a person who works at the apartment rental building walk by. Talk about being in the right place at the right time. In a matter of thirty seconds, the child went from extreme anxiety and fear to answered prayer and relief. God heard his cry, he opened the door, and he sent people on his path to help. Thank you, Jesus, for hearing the cry of your children. As believers, we have the key to someone's breakthrough. Jesus can open doors for others when you respond and pray.

Chapter 11

Growing in God

GOD FAITHFULLY KEEPS HIS *promises. He called you to be partners with his Son Jesus Christ our Lord*

1 Corinthians 1:9 GW

Many times we want to experience God is big miraculous ways. I'm very thankful for every miraculous experience he has given me. It is good to hunger for more of God and to see the supernatural things he has done. However, God is also found in all the little details of everyday life. It's important that we seek him first in everything we do and not just try to find him on special occasions, once a week, or during a conference.

Growing in Jesus

I grew up in a family of five. Mom, Dad, sister, brother, and me. Four of us had birthdays in December. My sisters birthday is December 9th, my brothers December 15th, the day after is my birthday December 16th, and my dad December 20th. We also celebrate the birth of Jesus, on December 25th. Even though my brother is three years younger than me, our birth days are just one day apart. Each year my parents would purchase a large cake for my brother and me to share. When I was young I enjoyed having cake on both December 15th, and then again on my birthday December 16th. However, as I got older I didn't want his cake leftovers. I wanted my own cake, with my own name on it, to celebrate on my own special day. I didn't want a cake that already had pieces missing. I wanted a new cake personalized just for me.

Celebrating another year of life is important. I believe birthdays are special not only to us but also to God. He knows the day you were born. He knows everything about your life. Yet, how much more special is it for us to celebrate the day we accepted Jesus Christ as our Lord and Savior. The day you were birthed into the kingdom of God! What a day of celebration that was. The day you were born again you became a child of the living God. That is a day to really celebrate.

> *"In the same way, I tell you, there is rejoicing in the presence of the angels of God over one sinner who repents." (Luke 15:10 NIV)*

When you asked Jesus into your life, the celebration had only just begun. Even the angels rejoiced. The days following that day would reveal God's goodness over and over, time and time again. The bible says that we are to "taste and see" that the Lord is good

Psalm 34:8 (NIV)

"Taste and see that the Lord is good; blessed is the one who takes refuge in him"

God has special plans for each individual life he created. God wants us to have our own personal relationship with him more than anything else. God wants to give us all our own "cake" so to speak. He has something special with your name on it, just for you. As young Christians, we may need to be spiritually fed by others in the family. Revelation, gifts, and insight can all be passed down to us from others and it can be sweet for a while. We may temporarily "taste" of the goodness of God by hearing the testimonies of others. However, as we mature in our relationship with Christ,

God wants each believer to individually taste of his goodness for themselves. He has a plan for your life that is personalized just for you. That is something to celebrate.

We can listen to teachings from others and appreciate Gods general word but there needs to come a time when we seek a word specifically for us as individuals. We must hunger to know what God is saying and not just generally, or overall, but what is he saying specifically for my life and for my situation?

God doesn't ask us to feed off of our brother's cake and blessings. Sure, I can be happy and celebrate with others in the family when they are blessed. However, there comes a day and a time when I just need to receive Gods blessings and Gods revelations for myself. We can and should taste of Gods goodness for ourselves. We can receive from God directly instead of hand-me-down revelations from others. Isn't that great! God wants to bless each person specifically, we just need to take refuge in him. Thank you, Jesus! There is nothing more important than taking the time to seek God for yourself. To taste of his goodness directly. To receive a word of revelation and understand the things he has prepared specifically for you.

Although wisdom gained from others can be sweet there is nothing sweeter than receiving a word of God for yourself. God wants each of us to taste and see for ourselves that He is good. He doesn't want us to be stuck feeding off of another person's blessings, gifts or "cake." God has blessings and gifts specifically for you with your name on it. You have spiritual food and it is found in the word of God. Father God has sweet things in store for each and every believer. The moment you were born into Gods kingdom, you became His child and only he knows what is best for each of His children. He has something special, something unique, a word, a calling, gifts, and a purpose for you alone. No one else can take that away from you.

Feast on the Word of God

Yes, there is a time to listen to testimonies that can build faith but there is also a time to step out in faith and say, I need my own testimonies too! God wants you to see for yourself, He wants you to taste for yourself. "Taste and see that the Lord is good" There is nothing sweeter than his Word spoken directly to your life and to your situation. He created you. God celebrates new life and personally rejoices in each of his children. We just need to take time and spend with him. Sit with him, seek him personally, and meditate on his word.

Oh, taste and see that the Lord is good!

Feast upon the promises God has given to you. Celebrate the life you have in Him, the blessings he gives are sweet indeed. Taste for yourself. See for yourself. God is good. You are blessed in him. You are unique and God has sweet things planned and personalized just for you! God makes all things new, a new year, a new you, new insight, new revelation, a new song and a new taste of his goodness. The Lord is good and blessed are those who take refuge in him. He has something prepared just for you and it is good. O taste and see. Amen

What treasure does God have for you?

"The kingdom of heaven is like treasure hidden in a field. When a man found it, he hid it again, and then in his joy went and sold all he had and bought that field"

Jesus often revealed the mysteries of his kingdom with the use of parables. He told stories to illustrate spiritual truths. Jesus would compare earthly things with spiritual things. He knew that many people would not be able to understand His parables. Jesus chose to speak in ways that only those who believe in Him could understand.

> *When Jesus was alone, "the twelve and the others around him asked him about the parables. He told them, "The secret of the kingdom of God has been given to you. But to*

those on the outside, everything is said in parables so that, "they may be ever seeing but never perceiving, and ever hearing but never understanding; otherwise they might turn and be forgiven!" Then Jesus said to them, "Don't you understand this parable? How then will you understand any parable?" (Mark 4:10–13)

The parables of Jesus are found in the books of Matthew, Mark, and Luke. I have come to understand that parables are often interpreted differently depending on who listens. Perhaps that is what Jesus wanted, He chose to share stories in a way that got people thinking. Supernatural encounters can do the same, no two encounters are alike. God speaks to each heart in a unique way with scripture, visions, dreams, and encounters.

Perhaps each response to his teaching would be different because each heart is different. Since the word of God is alive it has the ability to give each individual what they need. Parables have a way of revealing the thoughts of our heart and Jesus understood that. Supernatural encounters also have a unique way of revealing our hearts. Jesus speaks directly to you and He wants to know how do you interpret it? How does His Word spoken to you touch your life?

Chapter 12

Where is Your Treasure?

The Parable of Hidden Treasure

THERE ARE TEN SCRIPTURES in the book of Matthew that begin with the words "The kingdom of heaven is like." Jesus took a lot of time sharing the mysteries of the kingdom in a way that we could relate to. Apparently, Jesus wants us to think about the things of the kingdom because he taught on it frequently. Jesus is still sharing the mysteries of the kingdom with us today.

Let's look at Matthew thirteen verse forty-four.

> *"The kingdom of heaven is like treasure hidden in a field. When a man found it, he hid it again, and then in his joy went and sold all he had and bought that field" (Matthew 13:44).*

Immediately, upon reading this scripture I can see that the kingdom of God is priceless. The kingdom of God is hidden and it has more value than anything else. The kingdom of heaven is a treasure and who doesn't like treasure? Who wouldn't want to find that treasure? Yet is hidden and will take some seeking and searching to find. Anyone who finds a hidden treasure will be forever thankful for it.

To understand the scripture in more detail I began by researching the meanings of both the treasure and the field. I came across many different interpretations and possible meanings for each. One interpretation says "that the treasure is Christ, and the field is the Gospel. Another explanation says the treasure is salvation, and the field is the Bible. A third explanation is that the treasure is the Church, and the field is the world." While another believed that the treasure is the kingdom of Israel and the field is the entire human race.[1]

The more I researched, the more overwhelmed I became. How could it be? Just one verse in the word of God could have so many various interpretations and meanings. There were so many conflicting ideas being shared about possible meanings. No wonder Jesus said many would not understand his parables, they are secrets given only to his followers. Yet, even his followers seem to have differences of opinion.

So, in order to find the meaning of Matthew thirteen verse forty-four, I decided to seek the Lord for the answers myself, instead of leaning on the opinions of others. This is what the Lord spoke directly to me while in prayer. He simply asked me to look up the dictionary definition of the word field. After reading the definition for the word "field" I was given revelation knowledge on its scriptural meaning.

So often, when we read, "The kingdom of heaven is like a treasure hidden in a field." (Matthew 13:44a) we automatically focus on the treasure. Yet, God was asking me to begin my study by focusing on the importance of the word "field" instead.

The Field

According to the Oxford dictionary,[2] a field is "An area of open land, especially one planted with crops or pasture, typically bounded by hedges or fences." The first few words of the definition

---

1. Lindsay, The Life & Teachings of Christ Vol. 2, 117.
2. Oxford English Dictionary

really struck me, "An area of open land" God spoke to me again saying that, "His Kingdom is open to all." Everyone has been given an open invitation to enter the land of God's Kingdom. Some will accept his invitation to enter that field, while most others do not. Each person will have a personal choice to make if they are to enter his kingdom.

The next few words within the definition say, "especially one planted with crops or pasture" What a wonderful way to describe a field with "crops" and "pasture" both word choices are excellent in defining the kingdom of God. Why? Crops are harvested only when seeds have been sown, the word of God is like a seed. The seeds we plant on earth will ultimately bring a harvest of souls into Gods kingdom. The kingdom of God is like a field "especially one planted with crops or pasture."

A pasture is a green area of land suitable for sheep. Jesus is the good shepherd who laid his life down for the sheep (John 10:11). God's sheep will enter his pasture, his land, his field, we will enter his kingdom! Yes, the kingdom of God is an open land suitable only for his sheep.

The definition of "field" continued to amaze me. The definition ends with, "typically bounded by hedges or fences." Although the kingdom of God is open to all, there will be a boundary line and those that do not believe in Jesus will be unable to cross that line. Only by the blood of Jesus and the forgiveness of sins can one enter into Gods kingdom. All others will be bound and separated forever.

Perhaps the meaning of the field is exactly that, a field. An open area of land the kingdom of God is open to all who believe. We are invited into that land, and on our way to the kingdom we share the word of God, we sow the seed and he enjoys a harvest of souls. We are his sheep and we can rest in his pasture because it is open to us that follow him.

The Treasure and the Purchase

So, why did the Holy Spirit ask me to research the field before the treasure? I believe it is because of the following scripture. "For where your treasure is, there your heart will be also" (Matthew 6:21). So, the question is, "Where is your treasure?" The location of your treasure is very important. Is your treasure in the word of God? Is your treasure in Jesus? Do you treasure the things important to Gods kingdom? Do you treasure sowing the word of God and bringing in a harvest of souls? Where is your treasure located? The parable goes on to say "In his joy went and sold all he had and bought that field" (Matthew 13:44b). Are we prepared to give up everything in this life to follow Christ and gain entrance into His kingdom? Paul said, "What is more, I consider everything a loss because of the surpassing worth of knowing Christ Jesus my Lord, for whose sake I have lost all things. I consider them garbage that I may gain Christ" (Philippians 3:8).

Jesus said to Peter, "no one who has left home or brothers or sisters or mother or father or children or fields for me and the gospel will fail to receive a hundred times as much in this present age: homes, brothers, sisters, mothers, children and fields—along with persecutions—and in the age to come eternal life. But many who are first will be last, and the last first" (Mark 10:29–31).

We need to be willing to give away everything we have in exchange for his kingdom. We do not need to purchase our salvation however God does require that we invest in his kingdom. Will we value following him above all other things in this life? Do we see the treasure of his kingdom as being the most valuable thing we could have? How have you chosen to invest in his kingdom? When we understand the true value of the kingdom we will joyfully give up the things of this world. Nothing can compare to the great riches of his kingdom.

Jesus is worth more than anything we have and following him comes at a cost. In the parable, the one who found the treasure gave up everything he had so that he could gain something new. Likewise, we give up our own will and our old way of life, and we get a new life in exchange. God gives us a new life and entrance into his kingdom and that is more valuable than anything we could accumulate on earth. When we find Jesus we receive the treasures of the kingdom. Joyful treasures indeed.

What do you treasure most?

Jesus and his word are the greatest treasure anyone could ever find. His word will last forever. God wants us to treasure his word in our heart above everything else. We are also told to hide Gods word in our heart. (Psalm 119:11) Yes, the kingdom of God is like a hidden treasure. Jesus also said the kingdom of God is within you (Luke 17:21).

A parable challenges the listener to personal response and application. Each response can vary depending on the heart of the listener. Some take the time to seek its true meaning, while others may just skim over it and miss the meaning completely. The word of God is written for everyone. However, Jesus has the ability to teach different things to different people using the same parable. The only way you can truly hear what Jesus is trying to say, specifically to you, is to seek the Holy Spirit directly and not rely on someone else's commentary.

Just like the man in the parable realized that there was something infinitely more valuable than what he already possessed; we too, need to realize that the only treasure of any lasting value is found only in the kingdom of God and in Christ Jesus. The more time we take to seek him, the more treasure we will find and the more treasure we will have to share with others. "Oh, how I love your law! I meditate on it all day long." (Psalm 119:97 NIV)

Prayer

Jesus may we take time to study your word and find hidden treasures and revelations you wish to share with us personally. Help us to listen to your voice and seek your truth before seeking wisdom from others. Forgive me God for not spending enough time with you. Help me to prioritize my schedule so that I may seek you even more. Thank you, Jesus for sharing mysteries of the kingdom with me. Your word is priceless. Help me to hide your word in my heart that I may never sin against you Lord. Jesus, I treasure you and your word, there is nothing more valuable than you Jesus. Thank you, Lord Jesus, for speaking to my heart personally. I pray for more encounters with you and the Holy Spirit. Thank you, Jesus, for revealing truths of your kingdom as I read your word and encounter you in dreams and visions. Amen.

Chapter 13

Exchange Your Battle

"The Spirit of the Sovereign Lord is on me because the Lord has anointed me to proclaim good news to the poor. He has sent me to bind up the brokenhearted to proclaim freedom for the captives and release from darkness for the prisoners, to proclaim the year of the Lord's favor and the day of vengeance of our God, to comfort all who mourn, and provide for those who grieve in Zion— to bestow on them a crown of beauty instead of ashes, the oil of joy instead of mourning, and a garment of praise instead of a spirit of despair"

Isaiah 61: 1–3a New International Version (NIV)

THERE IS A DIVINE exchange that comes out of our weakness. Isaiah 61 tells us that God gives beauty for ashes, the oil of joy for mourning, and a garment of praise instead of a spirit of despair. We give our ashes to God and He gives us beauty! We give our despair to God and He gives us a garment of praise! We give Him our mourning, and He gives us supernatural joy. We give Him our rejection, He gives us His acceptance. We give Him our discouragement, He gives us his encouragement. God is constantly giving us beauty for ashes. What a beautiful relationship we have with Jesus.

We can trust in the Lord and hand him all aspects of your life. As we do this, He will transform us into a new creation. We will begin to see things differently. He will be our strength when we have none; He will be our joy in times of sorrow; He will be our hope when things seem dim, and He will pour out His power when we are weak. We give him our heart, He gives us his heart. We give Him our worries, He gives us rest. We give him our life, He gave us his life. We give Him our sins, He gives us forgiveness.

Whatever you're facing today, whatever hardship you have endured, whatever weakness you're fighting, give it to God and you will receive his power in return. Gods' power is made perfect in weakness. It is true. It is the word of God. Exchange your battle, your weakness, and let Him show you His power in return! The more hopeless a situation seems the more power you may experience. His power is made perfect in weakness. Give Him your weakness and His power will rest on you.

> *"My grace is sufficient for you, for my power is made perfect in weakness. Therefore I will boast all the more gladly about my weaknesses, so that Christ's power may rest on me."*
>
> *2 Corinthians 12:9 NIV*

I remember hearing testimonies of how this scripture had made powerful changes in many lives. Several people had addictions to smoking and had tried to quit for many years to quit and couldn't. They came to a point where they said I cannot, but God can. They had no power to change themselves, no matter how hard they tried they could not stop smoking, yet that is the best place to be. They had to be in a place of total weakness and complete trust and reliance on God to do what only God can. They said, "I can't, but God can" They praised God that they couldn't quit smoking because they knew God could take the smoking away from them. God is able. All things are possible with God. They were unable to quit, but God is able to make them quit. After they believed God is able to work, His power worked in their life and they never smoked again! They gave God their weakness, they received his power in return. "My grace is sufficient for you, for my power is made perfect in weakness."

After reading several testimonies I went to God in prayer myself, I told him exactly what I was struggling with. At that time I was battling a spirit of discouragement. I had been feeling discouraged and hopeless regarding a specific situation, I had done everything in my own strength to try and figure it out. My circumstances were screaming loss, and my mind was unable to process how it could possibly improve. Everything seemed to be falling apart, I didn't understand how God could make it any better. I had tried for many months to make it better, and there was nothing I could do. I had poured my heart into something God called me to do for years and it had come to an end. I was faithful but everything was changing. I didn't know how to cope with such a drastic change. I was uncertain of what the future would look like. What I was experiencing seemed to be a great loss to me, even my faith was being tested.

I prayed for Gods perspective to help me cope. I told God, "I can't see any hope in this situation, I'm unable to hope but God you are able to give me hope." The very next day, God spoke to my spirit and he turned things around for me. He gave me his perspective instead. Suddenly, what had seemed like a discouraging and hopeless situation turned into a very hopeful future and I was encouraged once again. Gods' perspective changes everything.

Gods Voice of Truth

When I woke up, God said, "I am expanding your territory" God had encouraged me as only he could. I had tried for months to understand what was going on in my life. There was so much change happening and suddenly God made sense of it all. God was not taking away everything as it had seemed, instead, he was bringing an increase!

God had bigger plans for me, and I could not have imagined them on my own. He had a new season for me, but I had to say goodbye to the previous season before I could experience it. He wasn't taking away, he was increasing. Thank you, Jesus, your power rests on me! Therefore I will boast all the more gladly about my weaknesses, so that Christ's power may rest on me."

Several months later God opened several new doors of opportunity for me. Yes, he had certainly increased my "territory" just as he had promised.

What are you struggling with today?

I'm confident that God can turn your situation around. God is able. His power is made perfect in your weakness. Honestly tell Him your weakness and his power will rest on you. Amen!

If we are willing to turn over a problem to God, then we can have faith that he will provide us with the answer. If we sincerely trust in him, He will answer our prayers. "He answered their prayers because they trusted in him" (1 Chronicles 5:20 NIV)

Let's put our trust in the Lord and hand him all aspects of our life. As we do this, he will transform us. We will begin to see things differently. He will be our strength when we have none; he will be our joy in times of sorrow; he will be our hope when things seem dim, and he will pour out his power when we are weak. Sometimes we just need a touch of heaven and to hear his voice.

Prayer

Lord Jesus, help me to hand my problems over to you. Thank you, Jesus, that you give me peace in this situation. I surrender my troubles to you and thank you that you exchange my weakness with your strength. Thank you that I can give you my burdens and you will give me rest. These burdens are not mine to carry. I trust you, Jesus, to help. Speak truth to my situation, help me to see this situation from your perspective. God, you are in control and I thank you for giving me wisdom. Thank you that I

Exchange Your Battle

can exchange my problems and receive your answers in return. In Jesus name, I pray. Amen.

2 Corinthians 12:9 NIV

"My grace is sufficient for you, for my power is made perfect in weakness." Therefore I will boast all the more gladly about my weaknesses, so that Christ's power may rest on me.

Chapter 14

Set Free to Set Others Free

GOD USES FLAWED PEOPLE. God works in our frailty and gives us the strength we need. We can step out in faith regardless of our ability. Look at how God used all these people in the Bible. Abraham was old, David was a murderer, Gideon was fearful, Job was bankrupt, Joseph was abused, Moses had a speech impediment, Martha worried, Naomi was a widow, Jonah ran from God, Peter denied Christ several times, and Zacchaeus was small. God will use anyone! God can take your painful past and use it for his glory.

Your test will turn into a testimony. Here are just some examples of what God can do.

> *"And we know that in all things God works for the good of those who love him, who have been called according to his purpose."*
> *(Romans 8:28)*

- A person was addicted to drugs. God turned their life around. Now they work in their dream job helping people who have also walked similar paths.
- Someone grew up in an alcoholic home. Jesus used that as a springboard to help them lead people out of bondage.

- A person was betrayed by a friend. They understand what it feels like to be stabbed in the back. Jesus turned their situation around and they become a counselor to others and share on the importance of friendships.

There are times in my life when the enemy tried his best to make me forget my purpose, there are times when he tried to remove the memories of God's goodness in my life. I must cling onto the scripture of Psalm 103:2, "Let all that I am praise the Lord; may I never forget the good things he does for me." Just like I can look at an actual photograph of memories, I can also recall the good things God has done for me. By memory, I can create my own God photographs of his hand at work in my life. Each story is a picture of God's grace in my life. Every memory shares a portion of his goodness, something I want to continually remember.

God watches over me every day of my life. God cares for me, He has been in every detail. He has transformed me, he has never left me, and he has never forsaken me. The Holy Spirit continually encourages me. That is what I want to share with you today. Memories, God memories. Everyday experiences, and encounters, moments that have shaped me into the person I am today. Memories that bring him glory. "Let all that I am praise the Lord; may I never forget the good things He does for me."

Romans 8:28 says "And we know that all things work together for good to them that love God, to them who are called according to his purpose."

If God has called me to help others walk in freedom than I need to be walking in freedom myself. I can only share what I know and what I have been given. Freely I've received so freely I give. Freedom can be a process. I didn't just wake up one day and see Jesus face-to-face. I went through a battle, cried out to him, and then he showed up. Life is not always a bowl full of cherries, there will be difficult days too. The point is that Jesus is with me every day no matter what I'm going through. I faithfully believe him and trust him even in the storm. Jesus has a way of appearing in the storm!

I want to praise God for personally setting me free from a spirit of rejection. It was something I carried around for many years. Once God set me free from rejection my outlook on life changed, even my countenance changed. After Jesus took away the rejection people came up to me at church and told me I looked different. They could see a visible change in the way I looked and carried myself. The healing was made evident even in my appearance. I was set free to help set others free. This is my testimony of how God transformed me.

Freedom from rejection, Transformed by God

Saturday evening (June 28th) I attended a revival meeting at Evangel Worship Center in North Carolina. At the end of the service, people were getting prayed for. I also decided to receive prayer. The prayer spoken over me that evening was spoken with such compassion. I remember being told how much God loves me and that I am very special to him. Then, God gave the person praying for me a word of knowledge that was very specific to me and my situation at the time. He said that I would begin to speak with boldness and that I wouldn't be timid anymore. Then the following words really touched my heart. He stated with a great deal of compassion that the "spirit of rejection" would not be bothering me anymore.

The way he spoke really touched my heart, he did not yell or raise his voice, and he didn't tell me I need to fight harder or pray harder to win or defeat anything. He just spoke with certainty and from a place of victory. He spoke as though I already won that battle, that the battle was already finished. I heard that I would no longer need to worry because the rejection was already gone, and it would no longer be a problem. Hearing that, I started to cry. When I heard that for the first time I would not be bothered by rejection I just cried out of absolute relief. I could feel the power of God touching me. I was so exhausted from such a lengthy battle and finally, that battle was over. I already had the victory.

At that moment I didn't need to stand strong or fight. I just sat down out of exhaustion and relief and started crying. The tears

I cried may have started out of sadness from things past but there was a shift as I felt God and the tears changed into tears of relief and thankfulness. I was so thankful that the victory was finally mine to have.

Sometimes God will send someone to pray for your breakthrough. I'm thankful for those prayers that day.

Change following a Healing Encounter

That day or rather that moment was all it took to heal me. The freedom that Jesus gave me was instant but walking it out with a new perspective took time. From that day forward it was up to me to continue walking in the victory I already have. Several situations came up within a few days after that meeting. However, I found myself responding differently to things that would have previously bothered me. On the Thursday following the meeting, the Holy Spirit spoke to me and said, "I want you to study scriptures on acceptance." The battle was won, but I was in the process of walking differently and renewing my mind, and thinking in a different way, as situations came up. God wanted to reassure me with his word, and he did a deep work in my heart. I began studying the word right away.

I read numerous scriptures on God's acceptance but when I got to one specific scripture it spoke so clearly to me that I once again began to cry. The Holy Spirit touched my heart and mind so deeply with the scripture of Romans 11:29.

Romans 11:29 *"For God's gifts and his call are irrevocable."* God's gifts and his call are irrevocable! He will never ever take away his gifts. His acceptance of me and my calling is irrevocable. I didn't need to work hard to earn his acceptance he simple accepts me for who I am.

What are some of God's gifts? What are the gifts he speaks of that with never be taken away? One is the gift of salvation. That means that I will always have a place with him. I will always have a home to go to. A home that will never be taken away from me. I am always welcome in his presence and never pushed out or pushed away. What a powerful word and such reassurance to me of his care and concern. I don't need to be perfect to be accepted. That means I can make one mistake, or two, or many mistakes and he will still welcome me always. I thank God for his grace and mercy.

The Bible is full of Gods promises, it is his will to give his children good and perfect gifts. (James 1:17) Gifts of salvation, gifts of healing, gifts of forgiveness, gifts of mercy, gifts of love, gifts of wisdom, gifts of comfort, gifts of instruction, gifts of correction, gifts of provision, and more. God continually gives good and perfect gifts to his children. He knows exactly what each of us needs and when it is needed. He is in control and his timing is always perfect.

God gave me a new key to use. It was a key to unconditional love and acceptance no matter what the circumstance may be. That is a gift that is irrevocable. God is Love that will never change and his love for me will never change either. I can't earn it, I don't deserve it but God loves me regardless. Hallelujah, Amen, Praise God!

There has been such a noticeable difference in my life since that day. I even had people walk up to me and tell me that I look like a different person. Even my very appearance had changed as I was set free from rejection. I looked like a new person because I was a new person. Transformed by God. It doesn't matter if you have been rejected by everybody else. You have been handpicked, chosen, and adopted by God.

A lesson I've learned

God loves me and accepts me. I already have victory over any battle I may have gone through. Start walking in victory because it is already mine to enjoy. Read the word of God and it will strengthen you. When God does an inner work of healing sometimes there can even be a visible difference in the appearance of a person. When God reveals the truth of his word in a person's heart, they are set free. Now I am more sensitive to others who are struggling. God will use my past to help encourage others for his glory.

Prayer

Thank you, Jesus, for loving me and for pulling me through such a tough time. Thank you, Holy Spirit, for helping me to remember that my life matters because it matters to Jesus. Jesus, you understand what it is like to go through difficulty. Thank you, Jesus you never left me. Thank you, God, for being there for me always. You will never leave or forsake me. Jesus, you're my best friend, Holy Spirit you are amazing. I love you, Jesus.

Thank you for your word, God. Thank you for the truth. Thank you for helping me and others to receive your truth and for setting us free with your truth. Thank you for words of life that strengthen us. Thank you for touching my life and for touching the lives of others. Thank you for wanting to use me to help others. Jesus may others see you in my life. Thank you that the calling on my life is irrevocable. Help me to walk in my calling and bring you glory Jesus. Thank you for your healing touch and for new chapters in my life. Amen

Chapter 15

Jesus Asks a Question

GOD WANTS US TO come before him as we are but with a sincere heart. He does not want us to put on a mask and hide our pain or try to handle our problems without him. God will use us even in our frailty. He wants us just as we are. What freedom we can experience knowing that we don't have to work for his attention or be perfect before he will listen to us. He knows our weakness, he knows our sin, he knows our struggles, and yet he still loves us. He is a loving Father and friend who just wants us to draw near to him with a sincere heart. He wants us as we are, not as we sometimes pretend to be. Invite the Lord into your life, seek him behind closed doors, and tell him the concerns of your heart. This is the personal relationship that he longs for.

Jesus Speaks

A personal relationship with Jesus includes our prayers to him but also his speaking to us. Today I heard Jesus ask me a question.
He said, "My child, why do you love me?"

Think about that question for a moment. First of all, would Jesus be able to address you as his child? Have you put your trust in God as your Father? That is an important question to ask. If your answer is yes, how would you respond to that same question?

Child, why do you love Jesus? Do you love Jesus? If so, why do you love Him? Think about your response for a moment and tell him your answer.

My answer is this, "I love Jesus because He first loved me. I love Jesus because he is always there for me, and he always listens to me. I love Jesus because he will never leave me. I love Jesus because he sacrificed his life for me. Thank you, Jesus, for being my friend.

Jesus is love. He loves us unconditionally. *"Give thanks to the Lord, for he is good; his love endures forever." (1 Chronicles 16:34 NIV)*

What would happen if I asked Jesus a similar question?

Jesus, why do you love me? His response would be different from mine. Jesus, why do you love me? He wouldn't reply "Because I am always there for Him (although I'm sure he wants me to always be there when he speaks). He would not say He loves me because I always listen to Him (even though he would always want me to listen to him). He couldn't say, I love you because you have never left me. However, I would like to think that Jesus would say that I am his friend. No, God does not love me because of what I do for him. He just loves me unconditionally, regardless of my behavior. I fall short in my relationship with him but he is faithfully there for me always. Nothing can separate us from Gods love. "How precious are your thoughts to me, O God! How vast is the sum of them! If I could count them, they would outnumber the sand." (Psalm 139:17–18a)

Neither height nor depth, nor anything else in all creation, will be able to separate us from the love of God that is in Christ Jesus our Lord. (Romans 8:39)

The Lord appeared to us in the past, saying: "I have loved you with an everlasting love; I have drawn you with unfailing kindness.

Jeremiah 31:3

God hungers to be close to us. He longs to speak to us. He thinks about us all the time. Yet, we all have sinned and fallen short of his glory (Romans 3:23), yet he is still loving and merciful to all. He does not favor the rich over the poor. He loves everyone equally no matter what we have done or where we have come from. He will never turn us away because of our past sin. He does not look at our past mistakes. God sees us as his wonderful creation and looks at us with loving eyes. We may not feel worthy to be loved by him, yet he loves us anyway. It is heartbreaking that we set aside only a little time for him when we know how much he truly loves us. He is always there to listen.

We come to him during church, or in times of need, but do we go home and continue to walk with him each day? I always want to feel the presence of the Lord. It is in his presence where all things are possible. It is in the yielding, and the praying, and the seeking, where his power is revealed. The more time we seek Jesus, the more we will encounter him. If you are looking to experience a supernatural encounter with Jesus just ask him for one and then spend time in his presence.

The Lord loves us all so much. We should show him the love and appreciation that he deserves. We tend to come to God only when we have a need, but we should continually praise him, and thank him, and tell him how much we love him, without bringing demands. How often do you praise him and thank him without asking for anything in return? He is worthy of our praise. Do you seek him only when there is an emergency?

Do you seek God as a provider and nothing more? Do you seek him only when you have a need? When Jesus asked the question, "My child, why do you love me?" I don't think he is looking for an answer such as, "I love you because of what you give me" Our relationship with God should not be selfish. If we only seek God when we need him, then we are putting limits on our relationship with him. He wants an ongoing relationship, not just one that calls him during a time of need.

The possibilities he has for our lives are far greater than what we can ask him for, or plan for ourselves. If we can only set aside our demands and realize that he is everything, then we will begin to see him work miracles on our behalf. We will experience a relationship with him, daily. That is what he is looking for.

Plans for the Future

"For I know the plans I have for you," declares the Lord, "plans to prosper you and not to harm you, plans to give you hope and a future."

Jeremiah 29:11 NIV

Someone once said that if you want God to laugh, tell him your plans. There is a lot of truth in that statement. We think we have all the answers and that we are in control. We set goals and we plan our future, but God already knows our future and his plans are greater than ours. If we want to have a prosperous future, we need to surrender ourselves to him completely. We need to have patience and allow him to direct us and guide us each day. We should not put demands on him to bless our lives. Rather, we need to make him our top priority and watch his blessings come naturally. *"Delight yourself in the Lord and he will give you the desires of your heart"* (Psalm 37:4 NIV).

We need to come to a point where we are willing to give our lives totally and completely to the Lord. *"For whoever wants to save his life will lose it, but whoever loses his life for me will find it"* (Matthew 16:25 NIV)

Reflect Jesus

I desire more of him and less of me. I want my life to reflect the love of Jesus. I want the Lord to use me as a tool for his purpose. I want to speak his word, not my own. The word of the Lord brings life, joy, and healings, but words of sin bring death and destruction. I want the words I speak, and the actions I take, to be what the Lord would have me to say and do. The more I seek him, the more I find him.

Do you hunger for the Lord? Do you want him to use you as a tool for his purpose? I encourage you to search your heart and pray to experience a deeper relationship with the Lord. After all, is said and done, the only thing of real importance is your relationship with him. Take some time and pray or write down some things you can praise God for.

He is worthy of our praise. Welcome his presence in your life. Continually welcome his presence in your life. If God is welcome in your life than you have a lot to be thankful for.

Surrender everything to God, be willing to hand everything over to him. Everything we have belongs to God anyway. We are so proud of our cars, our homes, our belongings, that we foolishly believe they belong to us. One flood, one hurricane, and everything we think we own could disappear in a moment notice. We must understand that it is God who has given us our health and the ability to work. He is our provider. Everything good thing we have is because of God. We want to take credit for the things we have accomplished, but we do not deserve this credit. We must give God the praise and credit for the things He has allowed us to have and to do. As we give God our life, we must give him everything—not just our belongings, tithes, or offerings, but our problems and concerns as well.

Jesus gave you his life. Now, are you willing to give him yours? Child of God, you can do nothing on your own. You have nothing to lose. You need God desperately. He will be there to guide you and encourage your every step of the way. All it takes to have the blessings of God enter your life is the willingness to call on his name. In the name of Jesus, all things are possible. May we walk in the power of the Holy Spirit and be living witness for his glory. Amen

Prayer

Jesus, I invite you into my life, into every area of my life. Help me to draw closer to you every day. I pray for supernatural encounters, visions, dreams, and revelation from your word specifically for me. Touch my heart as only you can. Holy Spirit fill me. Transform me into the person you called me to be and use my life for your glory. I thank you that the goodness of God will be made manifest in my life. Help me to set aside time to seek you and to treasure my time with you above all other things. Help me to shine the light of your truth everywhere I go. Give me opportunities to minister to those around me and to represent your kingdom. I thank you for helping me to effectively share the gospel with others. I thank you for speaking to me as I take the time to seek you. Use my life to speak the truth, your truth always. In Jesus Name I pray, The Glory belongs to God. Amen!

Bibliography

Lindsay, Gordon. *The Life & Teachings of Christ Vol 2*. Christ for the Nations Inc., 2010. (p. 117–118).

"Oxford English Dictionary." En.oxforddictionary.com Oxford University Press, 2019.<https://en.oxforddictionaries.com/definition/field/> (accessed 22 April 2019).

Toledo, Jennifer *"Children and the Supernatural"* Charisma House 2012 (p.38–40).

www.ingramcontent.com/pod-product-compliance
Lightning Source LLC
Chambersburg PA
CBHW070508090426
42735CB00012B/2692